A Search
for the
Spiritual

Also by James Emery White

Rethinking the Church

A Search

for the

Spiritual

Exploring Real Christianity

JAMES EMERY WHITE

This Billy Graham Evangelistic Association
special edition is published with permission
from Baker Book House Company.

BakerBooks
A Division of Baker Book House Co
Grand Rapids, Michigan 49516

Publishing by Baker Books
a division of Baker Book House Company
P.O. Box 6287, Grand Rapids, MI 49516-6287

Printed in the United States of America

Library of Congress Cataloging-in-Publication Data

White, James Emery, 1961–
    A search for the spiritual : exploring real Christianity / James Emery White.
      p.   cm.
    Includes bibliographical references.
    ISBN 0-913367-14-1
    1. Apologetics. I. Title.

For current information about all releases from Baker Book House, visit our web site:
http://www.bakerbooks.com

CONTENTS

ACKNOWLEDGMENTS

I am deeply indebted to countless individuals. Unfortunately, space allows the mention of only a few.

To my friends who have been, or are, seekers. Their questions and concerns, insights and challenges run throughout this book. Included in this group are the hundreds of seekers who come to Mecklenburg Community Church in Charlotte, North Carolina, each week to explore the Christian faith.

To three men—each having passed on from this life to the next—who have impacted my life and thought in various ways in regard to explaining Christianity to seeking minds and hearts: C. S. Lewis, Walter Martin, and Francis Schaeffer.

To my mother, Sue White, for being such an authentic spiritual seeker and imparting that to her son.

To my sister, Susan Ragsdale, who has read all my manuscripts before they have been published, giving trenchant criticism in the context of supportive encouragement. She possesses one of the brighter minds I have ever encountered, and all my writings are indebted to her. To Mark Mittelberg, who took time out of his busy schedule to give the book a careful read and offer invaluable advice.

To Paul Engle, my editor at Baker, goes great appreciation for being such a joy to work with and for championing this project from the beginning. To Melinda Van Engen, who once again provided a careful reading and sensitive editing. To Devlin McNeil, my assistant, goes nothing but praise for keeping my life in working order.

Finally, as always, the deepest thanks goes to my wife, Susan, who made every page possible.

THE BENEFITS
OF BECOMING
A SEEKER

For Mark, the issue was science. He liked stories that had an explanation, particularly an explanation based on observation. That's what made something believable. He wasn't an atheist; he just didn't think there was enough evidence to convince a person that any particular spiritual direction was correct.

Then his wife, along with a friend of his, invited him to a Christian church. Mark agreed to attend, but just to see if there *was* any evidence to support Christianity. Surprisingly, he found a setting in which he felt comfortable raising questions and searching for answers. His concerns were deemed valid; the issues he raised were never dismissed. He began to attend every Sunday, and then he joined a small group in which he was encouraged to talk openly and honestly about where he was in relation to God.

Over the course of a year, Mark came to two conclusions: First, he decided that no real contradictions exist between science and the Christian faith. Second, and on a more personal level, Mark came to grips with the fact that he was failing at life, unable to live up to even the simplest standards he

9

set for himself. Although the second issue was not part of his original search, the truth of it was inescapable. Mark decided he was in desperate need of leadership and that it could only come from God. Though he felt like he was jumping off a cliff, Mark became a Christian.

Kristi had been searching for years. Though raised in a non-religious environment, as a youth she occasionally went to church with her Catholic friends. For Kristi, when someone said they were a Christian, it was an instant turnoff because such a label was usually associated with a judgmental and intolerant spirit.

In her midtwenties, Kristi tried attending a church, but it was a disaster. The church was caught up in division and discord and eventually split. Kristi decided she wanted nothing more to do with the Christian faith, but what could only be described as a "spiritual hunger" began to invade her life. She felt a void that she desperately wanted to fill. She also wanted her little boy, Jackson, to have some kind of spiritual foundation.

Her seeking began again in earnest. She made a list of the things she wanted in a church, and she set off in pursuit. A believer in self-help books, she scoured the bookstore looking for material to help her in her search. She scanned the Internet, checking out sites on Christianity, Buddhism, Hinduism, Scientology, and the New Age Movement. She found no answers. Then two friends, both Christians, invited her to their church.

The first thing Kristi realized was that she was not, in fact, a Christian. Despite some previous involvement in a church, she had not in her heart of hearts truly accepted the leadership of Christ in her life. Then her husband, who had been attending with her, surprised her: *He* became a Christian. She felt cheated—after all, she was the one who had been searching! Then she came to a defining moment of personal insight: She had wanted to find God in order to add control to her life; she had never opened herself up to the possibility of finding

God in order to give up control of her life. Like her husband, Kristi found what she had been looking for and made the decision to order her life around Christ and become a Christian.[1]

Sociologist Wade Clark Roof recently released a book titled *A Generation of Seekers*. Based on his research of contemporary American culture, he concluded that the defining characteristic of our day is this: It is seeking.[2] But we're not searching for just anything. He believes we are *spiritual* seekers, with *spiritual* questions, looking for *spiritual* answers, trying to fill a *spiritual* void. We are looking for purpose and meaning in our lives.

We get up in the morning, go to work, come home, invest in our family or friends, and go to bed—and we don't know why. We don't know why we're working so hard, studying so hard, why we're married and trying to be committed to that marriage, or why we are working hard at being parents. We know why we're doing it on a superficial level—we work to make money, we study to make good grades, we stay married because we value commitment and it is often more practical to stay with one person over a long period of time, and we work hard at being parents because we love our children—but we don't know why we are living our life in an *ultimate* sense. It's tough to give, work, and sacrifice without knowing what it's all for in the end.

Where can we find purpose and meaning in life? No assembly line is going to manufacture a widget that brings purpose into our lives. Education isn't going to make it happen. The government can't do it. No piece of legislation or law will ever be passed that will address the state of my soul. It's as if we have finally realized that our deepest needs are spiritual in nature. As *Generation X* author Douglas Coupland has written,

> Here's my secret: I tell it to you with an openness of heart that
> I doubt I shall ever achieve again, so I pray that you are in a
> quiet room as you hear these words. My secret is that I need

God—that I am sick and can no longer make it alone. I need God to help me give, because I no longer seem to be capable of giving; to help me be kind, as I no longer seem capable of kindness; to help me love, as I seem beyond being able to love.[3]

Even with this realization, however, countless numbers of people never go into active search mode. It's as if they see their disease but never pursue the treatment. Søren Kierkegaard addressed this irony, telling about a make-believe country where only ducks live. On a Sunday morning all the ducks came into church, waddled down the aisle, waddled into their pews, and squatted. Then the duck minister came in, took his place behind the pulpit, opened the duck Bible and read, "Ducks! You have wings, and with wings, you can fly like eagles. You can soar into the sky! Ducks! You have wings!" All the ducks yelled "Amen!" and then they all waddled home.

For many of us, the spiritual dimension of our lives is like the wings of those ducks: It's there, we like hearing about it, we know it has enormous potential for our lives, but we never do anything about it!

We can begin to do something about it by examining the benefits of being a seeker.

You Pay Attention to Your Spiritual Life

As human beings, we are spiritual creatures. We are incurably religious. Though it may not manifest itself in a particular faith, the sense of our soul is compelling and real. As the French mathematician and philosopher Blaise Pascal noted, we have a God-shaped void in our lives that can only be filled by God.

As a seeker, you pay attention to your spiritual life. And once this happens, you begin to address the needs of your spiritual life, which is why the Bible records God inviting people to the search. For example, look at what God says through the prophet Jeremiah:

> "For I know the plans I have for you," says the LORD. "They are plans for good . . . to give you a future and a hope. . . . when you pray, I will listen. If you look for me in earnest, you will find me when you seek me. I will be found by you," says the LORD. "I will . . . bring you home again."
>
> Jeremiah 29:11–14 NLT

Seeking Helps You Keep an Open Mind

A second benefit that comes from being a seeker is that seeking helps you keep an open mind. If you never engage in the seeking process, then you have no idea if your current spiritual convictions, much less current spiritual state, are in alignment with ultimate spiritual truth.

I have a non-Christian friend who is a fairly well-known celebrity in the city in which I live. He is very outspoken in his denunciation of the Christian faith. I serve as an adjunct professor for a nearby seminary and invited him to talk to my students as to why he isn't a Christian. He was more than happy to do it.

It was an evening class, so my friend and I met for dinner, spent some time together, and then drove over to the campus, where he spoke for thirty to forty minutes about his life and background, his spiritual convictions, and why he isn't a Christian. Interestingly, most of his reasons were more emotional in nature than they were intellectual. He grew up as a Jew in the predominantly Christian South, and he was often ridiculed and rejected for his heritage, which made him less than receptive to the dominant faith of the region.

After his talk, he opened the floor for questions. The first question a student asked was simply, "Have you ever explored Christianity with an open mind as a seeker?" I thought to myself, "Good question." It was clear to my student, as it had been to me, that my friend's rejection of Christianity had less to do with its objective truth than with the wounding he had experienced as a boy.

He said, "No, I haven't, and I don't intend to."

The student just stared at him with his mouth open, then said, "Well, why?"

And my friend said, "I don't have to—I know it's not right, and I know I am."

During a phone call afterward, when my friend asked me how I thought it had gone, I said, "You know that I respect you as a person and respect your right to hold to your beliefs, but I need to tell you I was shocked to hear that you have never seriously explored Christianity yet are so open about rejecting it." He conceded that the concern was fair.

Only when you seek can you say that you are open-minded and that you have made a decision based on intellectual honesty. If you *think* you're right, if you *think* you know Christianity is false, but you've never checked it out, you really don't know.

You Figure Out Why
You Believe What You Believe

This leads to the third benefit of being a seeker: When you seek, you figure out why you believe what you believe. People believe what they believe for all kinds of reasons: the way they were raised, various experiences they have had, and the influence of important people in their lives, to name a few. These aren't bad reasons, but they can never replace the value and depth of holding to something because you went on a search for truth and found it.

When I was a young boy—just nine years old—it dawned on me one day that the reason I was a Christian was because my parents were Christians. It just hit me. I believed it all because

I had been raised to believe it all, told to believe it all, but that didn't make it true! If I had been born in India, I would have been raised to accept and believe in Hinduism. If I had been born in Iran, my parents would have raised me to accept the Islamic faith. I remember panicking. What if I hadn't been born in the right country? What if my parents hadn't raised me in the right faith? For whatever reason, I believed that spiritual truth was out there—somewhere—I just didn't want my geography to cause me to miss out on it.

> If you think you're right, if you think you know Christianity is false, but you've never checked it out, you really don't know.

So I went to my mother and said, out of the blue, "Mom, why are we Christians? Did you, like, check it out first? I mean, are we sure we're right on this?"

She gave me this look that said, "That does it. No more TV for this kid!" But she didn't blow me off, because the truth was that my mother had been a true spiritual seeker. She hadn't come to Christianity in a blind, mindless way. She took me seriously because she had taken her own search seriously. So she said something to me that was very unusual for a mother to say to her nine-year-old son. She said, "Jim, your father and I have looked at all the faiths of the world and have determined in our hearts and minds that Christianity is right—that Jesus really is the Son of God and that what he taught is true. But you have to come to that in your own mind. You're right. You shouldn't just take our word for it, so you are welcome to look into all the world's religions and come to your own conclusions."

When she said that to me, two things happened: First, I heaved a huge sigh of relief, not just because they had done their homework but because I was allowed to check it out too! There was something comforting about that, something reassuring. I could be sure. I could be confident. Those feelings about my faith were available if I wanted them.

The second thing our conversation did for me was put me into search mode. I really became a seeker. I began to think—for the first time—about my faith. I began to read the Bible. I asked questions. In the end, I decided I would stick with my parents' faith, not because it was their faith but because it was now *my* faith. I knew why I believed what I believed.

And it didn't end there. The freedom and encouragement I received to be a spiritual seeker during my boyhood served me throughout my teenage years and into college. There were countless times in my spiritual pilgrimage that I looked on the faith of my childhood and felt the freedom to put it on the firing line. My thoughts were always the same: If it's true, it will hold up. And I wanted to have a faith that is real, that I could believe in, that could stand up under any amount of scrutiny. When I actually made my life commitment to Christ as an adult, I knew what I was doing. I not only made the decision to embrace Christianity and give my life to Christ, I knew *why*.

When You Seek, You Can Find

The most important benefit of all is this: When you seek, you can find. This was Jesus' great invitation to seekers: "Ask and it will be given to you; seek and you will find; knock and the door will be opened to you. For everyone who asks receives; he who seeks finds; and to him who knocks, the door will be opened" (Matt. 7:7–8).

How to Explore Christianity Authentically 2

Christianity is the world's largest religious faith with 1.5 billion adherents around the globe. That's more than one out of every four people alive today. The birth of Jesus was so monumental that it split our reckoning of history into two parts: Everything that has happened on our planet took place "before Christ" or "after Christ." As Philip Yancey has observed, "You can gauge the size of a ship that has passed out of sight by the huge wake it leaves behind."[1]

If you are wanting to explore Christianity as a seeker, this book is for you. It not only attempts to explain the Christian faith, but it also tries to address the questions and concerns of seekers head-on. But it is only a resource—it shouldn't be the search itself. So let me suggest some things right at the beginning that will help you beyond the reading of these pages. These suggestions are not designed to manipulate you to accept the Christian faith but simply to help you check it out for yourself.

Maintain an Open Mind

First, decide that you're going to maintain an open mind. Sometimes we say we're going to explore something when we know that we are not really open to what we might find. Having an open mind doesn't mean blind acceptance of whatever you explore—you need to evaluate differing views, have some healthy skepticism, and check out the facts. What it does mean, however, is that you begin with an openness to what might be discovered. If you start off saying, "Yeah, I'll check it out, but I know it isn't true," then you're not exploring with an open mind. To seek authentically means that you keep a healthy balance between solid investigation and a willingness to accept what you find.

To begin your spiritual search with integrity, I suggest you begin with a seeker's prayer. Simply pray, "God, I am not even sure that I believe you're there listening to this, but if you are, I want to find you. I really do want to know the truth. If you exist, please show yourself to me."

Determine What It Is You're Looking For

Second, when exploring the Christian faith, determine what it is you're looking for, and make sure you have fair expectations. Most seekers would say they are after spiritual truth. They want answers to life's ultimate questions. They are looking for God and a relationship with God so they can order their lives accordingly. And that's fair. But people don't always stop there. Sometimes they tack on expectations that are not fair, such as "I want whatever I find to solve all of my problems—instantly." That isn't going to happen. Nothing works that way. Scott Peck wrote a well-known book called *A Road Less Traveled.* It opens with a line everyone can identify with: "Life is difficult." That's true. Life is difficult, and the Christian faith never promises it will deliver a life free of such difficulty.

The Bible teaches that when you give your life to Christ, your eternal destiny is altered, you experience a radical reorientation of your priorities, you find a new purpose in life, and you encounter the power and work of God in your life. But these experiences are far different from the instant removal of every problem, every struggle, or every issue of pain. Christians believe that the Bible says God can and does do miraculous, incredible things when you are in relationship with him, but that's not what you should look for, or what God always promises to deliver. Instead, God's power and presence, which come from being in relationship with him, give us the ability to go through the difficulties of life with strength and hope. "The good man does not escape all troubles—he has them too. But the Lord helps him in each and every one" (Ps. 34:19 TLB).

It is also unfair to want whatever it is you find to complement your lifestyle rather than change it. That's like saying, "I'd like to buy twenty dollars' worth of God—not enough to get me too excited or keep me up at nights, but just enough to make me feel good about myself."[2] Few religions, and Christianity in particular, allow for a mind-set that sees spiritual faith as an accessory item that does little more than enhance one's existing quality of life. Since your deepest needs and issues are spiritual in nature, you should expect your search to lead you to the deepest corners of your life, and you should expect what you find to change you from the inside out.

For example, take a look at what the Bible has to say about the nature of our interaction with God and his Word:

> For the word of God is full of living power. It is sharper than the sharpest knife, cutting deep into our innermost thoughts and desires. It exposes us for what we really are. Nothing in all creation can hide from him. Everything is naked and exposed before his eyes. This is the God to whom we must explain all that we have done.
>
> Hebrews 4:12–13 NLT

If you determine that God exists, you should anticipate that he can never be trivialized, marginalized, or put in a box. His truth is not designed to complement your life but to redirect it, change it, transform it.

Check Out the Source Documents

Once you've determined that you're going to search with an open mind, and you've got a handle on what is fair to expect from your search, it's time to begin the actual work of the search process. Begin by checking out the source documents of the Christian faith. The Bible is a collection of sixty-six books written by over forty authors over a period of several hundred years. Christians call it God's Word, or God's revelation to us. The word *revelation* comes from the Latin word *revelatio,* which means to "draw back the curtain." Christians believe that in the Bible God reveals himself and truth about himself that we could not otherwise know.

So the first thing anybody who is interested in the Christian faith ought to do is read the collection of documents that Christians claim is God's revelation. Interestingly, when Jesus was once asked a number of questions by a group of spiritual seekers, he answered them patiently, but finally, after diagnosing the flow of questioning, he said something intriguing: "You do not know the Scriptures. . . . Have you not read what God said to you?" (Matt. 22:29, 31). It was as if he were saying, "Listen, I'm more than happy to stand here and talk with you and answer questions, but it's becoming clear to me that you haven't even read the basic text!"

Here are two suggestions for you to keep in mind when reading the Bible. First, make sure you begin with a modern translation. Many seekers have tried to read the Bible but have found it difficult, obscure, and tedious—and for good reason! But the reason probably had less to do with the text itself than with the translation used.

The Bible was written in two languages: Hebrew and Greek. Hebrew was the language of the day when the Old Testament was written, and Greek was the language of the writers of the New Testament. As a result, all our Bibles today are translations of those original languages. When the Bible was translated in the 1600s, the Greek and Hebrew languages were translated into the language of that day: King James English. As a result, this version contains a lot of "thees" and "thous." The King James Version was an enormously popular translation because it reflected the language of the people of that day. But we don't talk that way today, and there's nothing magical or holy about King James English. Moses never said "heretofore" or "walketh," and neither did Jesus. That's the way people in the seventeenth century talked! I suggest you get yourself a good, modern translation that is easy for you to read and understand.[3]

Second, when reading the Bible, remember that it is really a library of books. You possess some freedom as to where to begin reading. In fact, I wouldn't start on page one and work my way through to the end. I know that's how we read most books, but it's not the best way to read the Bible. Most people who are familiar with the Bible would suggest that you start with one of the four biographies of the life

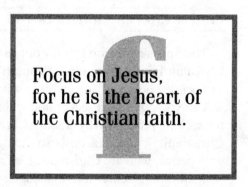

Focus on Jesus, for he is the heart of the Christian faith.

of Jesus found in the books Matthew, Mark, Luke, and John (named after the men who wrote them). These books will lay a good foundation of the central message of the Bible—Jesus and his life and ministry. After that, go to the Book of James, which is a practical little book containing five chapters that will show you what patterning your life after Christ might look like. Then read the first book, Genesis, in which you'll find answers to some of the foundational questions of human existence in light of what you've learned about Christ. After that, you're probably in good shape to jump in wherever you want.

Come to Terms with Jesus

My fourth suggestion involves the focus of your search. Focus on Jesus, for he is the heart of the Christian faith. When I say "focus on" him, I mean that you should come to terms with his identity.

Here we have a man who walked the earth and claimed to be equal to God. No other major religious figure ever made that claim—not Buddha, not Mohammed, not Confucius. Only Jesus Christ claimed to be God in human form. Was he or wasn't he? This is the ultimate question a spiritual seeker must answer when it comes to the Christian faith.

Find a Church That Lets You Seek

The final suggestion I throw out to you as you explore the Christian faith is this: Find a church that will let you start exploring where you are. In other words, find a church that will let you come as a seeker and will attempt to help you in the seeking process. Why attend a Christian church to explore Christianity? One reason is so that you can talk firsthand with people who are Christians. Listen to their stories, raise your questions, enter into a dialogue with them about their faith. Some churches, such as the one I pastor, even have services and small groups designed for spiritual seekers. You might be surprised at how many churches are not only open to your search but willing to serve it.

Your search is the most important search in the world. In truth, there's no such thing as a "spiritual life"—there's just "life," and your spirituality courses through its every vein. Thus, finding the door to spiritual truth, opening it, and walking through it make up the most significant journey you can ever undertake, for on the other side is not simply spiritual life, but life itself.

IS SOMEBODY OUT THERE?

On August 7, 1961, a twenty-six-year-old Russian cosmonaut became the second Soviet to rocket into space, orbit the earth, and return safely. After he returned, he sarcastically let it be known that he had looked for God but had not seen him. He concluded that God did not exist.

Lee Strobel could identify. He was an atheist with a fulfilling and financially rewarding job as the legal affairs editor at the *Chicago Tribune.* He saw little need for God—in fact, he was hostile to church and to spiritual things. He felt that the very idea of God was ridiculous, so much so that it was not even worth investigating. But then his wife became a Christian through a church that presented the Christian faith in a way that made sense. She encouraged her husband to come and check it out. Reluctantly, Lee agreed, but to make sure no one thought he was actually interested in God, he carried his reporter's notebook with him so he could claim he was just working on a story.

Lee's first visit led to another, and then another, and soon— though an atheist—Lee began to explore Christianity. He used his legal and journalistic skills, background, and training to explore and investigate the evidence of the Christian faith. He looked at historical evidence, circumstantial evidence, biblical evidence, and ancient writings. He explored world religions, philosophical discussions surrounding Christianity, and prophetic evidence. Then, after twenty-one months, he came to a startling conclusion: It would take a lot more faith *not* to believe in God than *to* believe in God. Lee began to follow this newly discovered God, and it changed his life, so much so that his then five-year-old daughter went to her mother and said, "I want God to do for me what he did for my dad."[1]

There aren't too many card-carrying atheists in America. Recent polls show that 74 percent of all Americans strongly believe in the existence of a God who is holy and perfect and who created the world and rules it today.[2] Some polls place that figure as high as 96 percent.[3] There are, however, quite a few agnostics. An agnostic doesn't necessarily reject God as much as the possibility of knowing whether God exists. Rather than saying, "I *don't* know whether there is a God," an agnostic says, "I *cannot* know whether there is a God."

It is true that you cannot put God in a test tube for examination. You cannot prove that God exists, at least not by normal scientific methods. The scientific method depends on repetition, and there are certain things that cannot be contained or repeated. If something is

> Seekers should look for evidence that supports whether it is *reasonable* to believe in the existence of God—signs, if you will, of his existence.

beyond your five senses, you cannot use science to either prove or disprove it. But just because you can't prove something scientifically doesn't mean it isn't real. No one has ever seen love, but we all know it is real. No one has ever smelled freedom, but it exists. And, of course, God—by almost any definition—would be very hard to examine using human means. So instead of looking for a chemical reaction in a test

tube that would somehow reveal God's existence, seekers
should look for evidence that supports whether it is *reasonable* to believe in the existence of God—signs, if you will, of
his existence. Christians believe that such evidence exists in
abundance, beginning with an observation as simple as cause
and effect.[4]

Cause and Effect

Most of us have ventured out on a summer's night and
gazed up at the stars. During those moments, we naturally
reflect on how the vastness of the universe came into being.
Until recently, the idea that the world was created by a personal God was dismissed by many as intellectually absurd.
The late astronomer Carl Sagan began his best-selling book
Cosmos by saying, "The cosmos is all that is or ever was or
ever will be."[5] Yet the second law of thermodynamics states
that the universe is running out of usable energy. If the universe is running out of energy, it cannot be eternal. It must
have at one time been given an initial start of energy. Something does not "wind down" unless it has been "wound up."

This idea has been supported by the leading hypothesis
for the beginning of the universe called the big bang theory.
As first articulated by Dr. Edwin Hubble, it maintains that at
one time all matter was packed into a dense mass at tem-
peratures reaching many trillions of degrees. Then, roughly
four billion years ago, a huge explosion took place. From that
explosion, all the matter that today forms our planets and
stars was born. And in what has been called the discovery of
the century, the Cosmic Background Explorer satellite, better known as COBE, has provided stunning confirmation of
the big bang creation event.[6] The startling conclusion is that
the universe did not always exist.[7]

Why is this so significant? Simply put, if the universe had
a beginning, then it must have had a cause. Imagine seeing

a row of dominoes falling over. It would be reasonable to assume that since they are falling over, somewhere, somehow, an initial domino was pushed. If the universe is not eternal, then at some point something that was independent and separate from the universe began the process. The great cosmological question is "What caused the big bang?" No wonder that on April 24, 1992, when the COBE satellite had measured the ripples in the microwave background radiation that gave confirmation to the big bang theory, Dr. George Smoot, head of the COBE satellite team, noted that it was "like looking at God."[8] Dr. Robert Jastrow, professor of astronomy at both Columbia University and Dartmouth College, director of the Mount Wilson Institute and manager of the Mount Wilson Observatory, and for twenty years director of NASA's Goddard Institute for Space Studies, made the following comment in regard to the COBE findings: "Now we see how the astronomical evidence leads to a biblical view of the origin of the world."[9]

The big bang theory not only raises the question of cause but also content. It's not simply a matter of what caused the universe to "bang" into existence but what it was that "banged." While the big bang theory holds that the universe we now observe emerged from an explosion some ten to twenty billion years ago, the theory also assumes that all the matter in the universe was present from the start. Since it is understood that something cannot be created from nothing, there is no scientific explanation for the actual origin of the matter of the universe. To raise the stakes even higher, the 1970 paper on black holes that vaulted Stephen Hawking to fame, written with Roger Penrose, theorized that at the moment of the bang, the laws of science did not even exist, raising the provocative question, "How did the laws of science come into existence?"[10] Physicist Alan Guth agrees, noting that even if a plausible theory could be constructed that could account for the creation of something from nothing through the laws of physics, one would still have to account for the origin of the laws of physics.[11] Such considerations have led Robert Jastrow to make the following confession:

> For the scientist who has lived by his faith in the power of reason, the story ends like a bad dream. He has scaled the mountains of ignorance; he is about to conquer the highest peak; as he pulls himself over the final rock, he is greeted by a band of theologians who have been sitting there for centuries.[12]

But Christians point to far more than cause and effect for evidence of the reality of God.

On Design and Order

Imagine you came upon a space shuttle in the desert. You could reason that it came together by chance: The metal was flung together by way of a chaotic sandstorm; the instruments and panels and wings were brought together by a freak accident of nature. But it is highly unlikely that this would be your first thought. If you came upon a space shuttle in the desert, your initial thought would likely be that someone made it and placed it there.

The intricate design of the universe has long stimulated the minds of spiritual seekers in a similar fashion.[13] The thinking goes as follows: All designs imply a designer. Buildings imply an architect, paintings suggest a painter. There is design in the universe. As a result, it is reasonable to assume that there is a Great Designer. William Paley used a watch for his point:

> In crossing a heath, suppose I pitched my foot against a *stone,* and were asked how the stone came to be there; I might possibly answer, that, for any thing I knew to the contrary, it had lain there for ever. . . . But suppose I had found a *watch* upon

the ground, and it should be inquired how the watch happened to be in that place; I should hardly think of the answer which I had before given. . . . When we come to inspect the watch, we perceive (what we could not discover in the stone) that its several parts are framed and put together for a purpose. . . . The inference, we think, is inevitable, that the watch must have had a maker . . . who comprehended its construction, and designed its use.[14]

The alternative is that infinite time plus chance, in the context of chaos, created incredible order and purpose. One-time Plumian Professor of astrophysics at Cambridge University, Sir Fred Hoyle, has determined that if you would compute the time required to get all 200,000 amino acids for one human cell to come together by chance, it would take about 293.5 times the estimated age of the earth, which is usually set at around 4.6 billion years.[15] This would be akin to having the software for the latest windows application result—by chance—from an explosion in a computer warehouse.

Even further, Hoyle, along with his colleague Chandra Wickramasinghe, calculated the odds for all of the functional proteins necessary for a one-cell animal to form in one place by random events. They came up with a figure of one chance in 10 to the 40,000th power—that's 1 with 40,000 zeros after it! Since there are only about 10 to the 80th power atoms in the entire universe, Hoyle and Wickramasinghe concluded that this was "an outrageously small probability that could not be faced even if the whole universe consisted of organic soup."[16] Physicist Stephen Hawking once told a reporter that "the odds against a universe like ours emerging out of something like the big bang are enormous. . . . I think clearly there are religious implications."[17] Going even further, Hawking conceded that "it would be very difficult to explain why the universe should have begun in just this way, except as the act of a God who intended to create beings like us."[18]

This has led to what some have called the anthropic principle, namely that our world is uniquely suited to human
beings and the rise of carbon-based life, which is the only
known form of life. In a National Public Radio interview,
Owen Gingerich, professor of astronomy and the history of
science at the Harvard-Smithsonian Center for Astrophysics
in Cambridge, noted that "there are so many wonderful
details which, if they were changed only slightly, would make
it impossible for us to be here, that one just has to feel, somehow, that there is a design in the universe and, therefore, a
designer to have worked it out so magnificently."[19] Or as
theoretical physicist Paul Davies of Cambridge has observed,
"We are meant to be here."[20]

Regardless of the odds, the complex design of the world
has been explained in nonsupernatural terms—at least in
terms of the existence of life—through Darwinian evolution.
As biochemist Michael Behe explains, "For more than a century most scientists have thought that virtually all of life, or
at least all of its most interesting features, resulted from natural selection working on random variation."[21] The Darwinian idea is that an incremental, step-by-step process is
what produced plants and animals in the first place, including the existence of such complex organs as the eye. The
argument is that while it may appear that there was an atten-
tive watchmaker who designed the complexity of the world
and its inhabitants, it was the blind watchmaker of evolution
that caused nonliving matter to produce all of life in its complexity by entirely natural means.[22] So the complexity of the
eye is simple to explain: You begin with a light-sensitive spot,
then through a process of random genetic changes and natural selection, you gravitate toward a group of cells that are
cupped to focus light better, and on and on the process goes
through a series of gradual improvements until you have a
true lens and the wonder of the human eye.

Yet Darwin himself noted that "if it could be demonstrated
that any complex organ existed which could not possibly have

been formed by numerous, successive, slight modifications, my theory would absolutely break down."[23] Biochemist Michael Behe has taken up Darwin's challenge and speaks to it in terms of a mousetrap. The common mousetrap includes a platform, hammer, catch, spring, and holding bar. Each component is required for the mousetrap to function as a mousetrap. You cannot start with a wooden base and catch a few mice, add a bar and catch a few more, and functionally evolve—step by Darwinian step—into the most effective mousetrap, which has a base, hammer, spring, catch, and holding bar. In order to even begin functioning as a mousetrap, there must be a minimum number of interacting parts assembled that allow the catching of mice to begin developing into more advanced levels of mice catching. This is what it means to be "irreducibly complex," to be a system that consists of several interacting parts that must be in place in order to function as that system.

Darwinian evolution depends upon there being a minimal function in place from which the more advanced functions could evolve. But as an "irreducibly complex" system, our mousetrap could not have been produced by continuously improving an initial function of mouse trapping by slight, successive modifications of the mouse-trapping process. Take away any of the five parts, and no mice would be caught![24] The conclusion is that the mousetrap was somehow made as an intact system. It could not have evolved into that system; it had to have been designed—as a system—for that purpose.

And this is the new and astonishing conclusion of molecular biology: The basic forms of life are not simple but irreducibly complex molecular machines that cannot be explained by natural selection working on variation. Vision, for example, is such an irreducibly complex organic system that it could not have appeared gradually in a series of small steps. For the lens of the eye to develop, there had to have been a light-sensitive spot from which the lens evolved. But

a light-sensitive spot is "irreducibly complex," meaning that
the complex molecular systems that together form that light-
sensitive spot could not have evolved because prior to that
interaction, there was no light sensitivity in place from which
to evolve![25] Behe, as a biochemist, concludes that the result
of recent research into life at the molecular level is a loud,
piercing cry of intelligent design.[26] No other explanation
exists for the incredible complexity of the world. But something even more intricate than the human cell raises the
necessity of God in the minds of countless seekers: the human personality.[27]

Human Personality

Beyond our physical bodies is the reality of human personality. As human beings we are able to think, reflect, feel,
and reason. It is difficult to believe that the human personality—the soul, if you will—evolved unaided from a pool of pri-
mordial slime. That which is inside of me, that which makes
me *me,* the voice inside my head when I think my thoughts—
where did these things come from? The origin of human personality becomes even more intriguing as a result of our innate
spirituality. Anthropologists have discovered that human
beings are incurably spiritual and conscious of the idea of
God. As Augustine reflected, "You [God] have made us for
yourself, and our hearts are restless until they rest in you."[28]

Human "drives" supposedly come about due to the reali-
ties of the world. We have an appetite for food, and there is
food to satisfy that need. We have an appetite for sex, and we
are able to enter into sexual relationships to satisfy that drive.
Within each of us is an authentic spiritual hunger. If there was
no real reason for us to believe in God, no way to satiate the
desire, why would the idea of God be such a universal phe-
nomenon throughout time and history? Why would creatures
who evolved from a molecular soup kitchen independent of

a Creator desire and hunger after that which has no place in their reality? One could argue that it is simply our desire for a God that creates such drives. This was Freud's belief, but it fails to explain the universal nature of the human desire for God throughout time and across civilizations.[29] At some point, particularly in our modern context, one would think that the wish for God would simply end. Yet it only grows.

Coupled with this is our inner sense of morality. Intuitively, each of us appeals to some sense of right and wrong in our dealings with ourselves, with others, and with the world. We get up from our seat on a crowded bus, someone sits in our place, and we say, "Hey, that's my seat! I was there first!" When we do that, we are appealing to some behavorial standard that the other person is supposed to know and accept. And there is a surprising consensus from civilization to civilization, culture to culture as to what is right and what is wrong. If you studied the moral teachings of the ancient Egyptians, Babylonians, Hindus, Chinese, Greeks, and Romans, you would be amazed at how similar they are to each other. For example, selfishness has never been admired, and loyalty is always praised. Men may have differed as to whether one should have one wife or fourteen, but they have always agreed that a man must not simply have any woman he liked.[30] As C. S. Lewis once observed, "My argument against God was that the universe seemed so cruel and unjust. But how had I got this idea of *just* and *unjust?* A man does not call a line crooked unless he has some idea of a straight line."[31] Somehow it seems that we have an innate sense of right and wrong. As Mark Twain once wrote, "Man is the only animal that blushes." Where does this come from independent of an outside source?

It's Your Choice

In the 1850s, the German philosopher Friedrich Nietzsche proclaimed, "God is dead." During the 1960s, someone spray painted "God is dead," and signed it "Nietzsche" on a bill-board near Union Seminary in New York. Someone else, undoubtedly a seminary student, took a can of paint and wrote, "Nietzsche is dead," and signed it "God." This question of God's existence has been the subject of more debate than any other question.[32] The only question that could match its significance is built on it: If God exists, what is he like? The Christian answer might surprise you.

WHAT IS GOD LIKE?

4

I f you are open to believing in God, the next question is clear: What is God like?

I once heard about a little girl who was drawing a picture at school. Her teacher came over and asked her what she was drawing.

"I'm drawing a picture of God," she said.

Her teacher said, "Honey, you know, nobody really knows what God looks like."

The little girl replied, "Well, they will when I get through!"

Most of us have a picture of God in our minds that we have drawn based on ideas, feelings, and experiences from our lives. Christianity presents a picture of God that is both unique and compelling, but it may be quite different from the picture you've established. George Buttrick, former chaplain at Harvard, recalls that students would come into his office and say, "I don't believe in God." Buttrick would then reply, "Sit down and tell me what kind of God you don't believe in. I probably don't believe in that God either."[1]

The Cosmic Cop

Some images portray God as a cosmic cop, a being whose mission in life is to catch us doing something wrong in order

35

to punish us. His interaction with us is all about law and order. If we play by his rules, he'll probably leave us alone. If we step out of line—even a little—he is ready and waiting to press charges. God as the cosmic cop is stern, strict, severe, unfeeling, and by-the-book. His fundamental attitude toward us is one of anger, and he's just waiting for us to violate his code so that he can slap on the cuffs.

This is not, however, the God of the Bible. There is no doubt that God is a God of justice and truth, right and wrong, but that's not all there is to him, and the way those characteristics and attributes are manifested does not correspond with the label cosmic cop.[2] The Bible says that "the LORD is compassionate and gracious, slow to anger, abounding in love" (Ps. 103:8). The prophet Isaiah talked about God in terms of a nurturing mother, caressing and holding and caring for us as a child (Isa. 66:13). Throughout the Bible countless references are made to God's tenderness, his patience, his sensitivity to our weaknesses, and his desire to be a friend. The idea of God as stern, rigid, and insensitive to our weaknesses is simply not the God of the Christian faith. Instead, the Bible tells us that

> he doesn't punish us
>   as our sins deserve.
> How great is God's love for all
>   who worship him?
> Greater than the distance
>   between heaven and earth! . . .
> Just as parents are kind
>   to their children,
> the LORD is kind
>   to all who worship him,
> because he knows
>   we are made of dust.
>   Psalm 103:10–11, 13–14 CEV

The Celestial Santa Claus

Some people picture God as a celestial Santa Claus, a grandfatherly type who smiles at everything we do and then pats us on the head while giving us whatever it is we want. This picture of God is safe, comfortable, convenient, warm, and fuzzy—regardless of how we live—because even though we are told that Santa Claus knows who has been naughty or nice and that there are implications for both types of behavior, Christmas always comes. Santa is simply too nice and jolly to do anything else!

According to the Bible, this is every bit as distorted as seeing God as the cosmic cop. It may be who we would like God to be so that we can live however we want without having to deal with the consequences, but it's not who the Bible says God really is.

In his classic children's tale *The Lion, The Witch and the Wardrobe,* written as a Christian allegory, C. S. Lewis uses Mr. and Mrs. Beaver to introduce the great lion Aslan of Narnia to four young children:

"Who is Aslan?" asked Susan.

"Aslan?" said Mr. Beaver. "Why, don't you know? He's the King. He's the Lord of the whole wood, but not often here, you understand. Never in my time or my father's time. But the word has reached us that he has come back. He is in Narnia at this moment. He'll settle the White Queen all right. It is he, not you, that will save Mr. Tumnus."

"She won't turn him into stone too?" said Edmund.

"Lord love you, Son of Adam, what a simple thing to say!" answered Mr. Beaver with a great laugh. "Turn *him* into stone? If she can stand on her two feet and look him in the face it'll be the most she can do and more than I expect of her. No, no. He'll put all to rights . . ."

"But shall we see him?" asked Susan.

"Why, Daughter of Eve, that's what I brought you here for. I'm to lead you where you shall meet him," said Mr. Beaver.

"Is—is he a man?" asked Lucy.

"Aslan a man!" said Mr. Beaver sternly. "Certainly not. I tell you he is the King of the wood and the son of the great Emperor-Beyond-the-Sea. Don't you know who is the King of Beasts? Aslan is a lion—*the* Lion, the great Lion."

"Ooh!" said Susan. "I'd thought he was a man. Is he—quite safe? I shall feel rather nervous about meeting a lion."

"That you will, dearie, and no mistake," said Mrs. Beaver. "If there's anyone who can appear before Aslan without their knees knocking, they're either braver than most or else just silly."

"Then he isn't safe?" said Lucy.

"Safe?" said Mr. Beaver. "Don't you hear what Mrs. Beaver tells you? Who said anything about safe? 'Course he isn't safe. But he's good. He's the King, I tell you."[3]

The prophet Isaiah was one of the holiest men of his generation. He was the spiritual leader of his day and was deeply revered. He had an authentic relationship with God. The Bible records that Isaiah had an experience in which he actually encountered the living God. It is interesting to note how this holy man in a good relationship with God responded to the actual *presence* of God:

In the year that King Uzziah died, I saw the Lord seated on a throne, high and exalted, and the train of his robe filled the temple. Above him were seraphs, each with six wings: With two wings they covered their faces, with two they covered their feet, and with two they were flying. And they were calling to one another:

"Holy, holy, holy is the LORD Almighty;
the whole earth is full of his glory."

At the sound of their voices the doorposts and thresholds shook and the temple was filled with smoke.

"Woe to me!" I cried. "I am ruined! For I am a man of unclean lips, and I live among a people of unclean lips, and my eyes have seen the King, the LORD Almighty."

Isaiah 6:1–5

That's not a response you'd give to a benign, grandfatherly Santa Claus, but it is the response you would give to the God of the universe. Safe? No, but good.

The Tyrannical Ruler

Another common perception of God is that of a tyrannical ruler, a demanding despot before whom we must grovel and cower in submissive fear. This God can be appeased, but only through a life of servitude. The tyrannical ruler does not exist to serve but to be served.

This is not, however, the God of Christianity. The Bible says that when you come to God for a relationship through Christ, you are adopted by God into his family. He becomes your Father, not your dictator, and you become his son or daughter, not his slave. When you come to God through Christ, you aren't given marching orders and told to fall into line, you become a member of his family. You are dearly loved and prized, the recipient of God's special affection. That's why the Bible says,

> For all who are led by the Spirit of God are children of God. So you should not be like cowering, fearful slaves. You should behave instead like God's very own children, adopted into his family—calling him "Father, dear Father."
>
> Romans 8:14–15 NLT

The Big Man

Some pictures of God have less to do with his character than with his nature. One such picture presents God as a "big man," sort of a John Wayne figure who is like us but bigger and better. I watched the beginning of one of Wayne's movies a while back. It was called *Cahill: U.S. Marshall.* The opening of the movie was classic John Wayne. He comes up— alone, of course—on five heavily armed outlaws. Looking them in the eye, he says something along the lines of, "Boys, I hear you robbed the bank. I'm here to bring you in. Are you ready to surrender?"

They all start laughing. Then one of them says, "Surrender? There's five of us and only one of you."

"Yep," John says, "that's about the size of it. So does that mean you're gonna surrender or not?"

Then, with a signal from their leader, the outlaws reach for their guns, but John whips out his rifle and bags every one of them. The next scene shows John riding off with all five men draped over their horses. Now that's a man—a *big* man.

A lot of people tend to think that's what God is like: a very big, very strong, very advanced person. But according to the Bible, that's not a true picture of God. While God is a person and is personal, he is not a human being, or even an advanced human being. Instead, the Bible says that "God is spirit" (John 4:24), "the King eternal, immortal, invisible, the only God" (1 Tim. 1:17). While the Bible often uses physical imagery as a means of explaining the personality of God (e.g., many of us grew up singing "He's got the whole world in his hands"), God is not made of flesh and blood. His nature and being go far beyond an advanced, superhuman version of ourselves. While the characters played by John Wayne were often strong and noble and good, they weren't all-powerful, all-noble, or all-good. His characters had limitations that resulted in weaknesses and failure. But the God of the Bible is totally perfect and complete in every way, which means

> **The God of the Bible is totally perfect and complete in every way, which means that God can be trusted and counted on in ways that go beyond our human limitations.**

that God can be trusted and counted on in ways that go beyond our human limitations.

The Force

While some images of God are too human, some are not human enough. The *Star Wars* movies have proven to be some of the most popular movies in history. In 1997, twenty years after its debut, the trilogy was rereleased to packed houses. In the first movie, Luke Skywalker meets an old man named Obe-Wan Kenobi, who was a Jedi Knight. Obe-Wan gives Luke his father's lightsaber and instructs him in the ways of the force. He tells young Luke that the force is what gives a Jedi his power. It's an energy field created by all living things. It surrounds us and penetrates us, binding the galaxy together. Obe-Wan also tells Luke that the force has a good side and a dark side and that he must beware of the dark side.

Some people picture God in a similar manner. *Everything* is God. All things partake of one divine essence, and that great oneness is called God. God is not a "he" but an "it"— a principle, a life force, a consciousness, an energy. Since we partake of this divine energy field, we *are* that energy field. The actress Shirley MacLaine has popularized this idea of God. At the climax of the TV movie in which she portrayed herself, she is seen running on the beach, exclaiming, "I am God! I am God!"

Christianity, however, contends that this is a misrepresentation of the true nature and identity of God. The Bible does teach that God surrounds and guides the universe and that he is present everywhere. He *is* Spirit, but that's where the similarity ends. Notice, for example, how the Bible talks about the creation of the world and human beings: "In the beginning God created the heavens and the earth. . . . God created man in his own image, in the image of God he created him; male and female he created them" (Gen. 1:1, 27). We are personal beings, and we have that personality because we were made in the image of God, who is personal. This is the very basis of Christianity: God is person and wants to be in a personal relationship with every one of us.

The Real God

One of the most famous declarations of spiritual guidance is known as the Ten Commandments, recorded in the Book of Exodus in the Old Testament. Each commandment provides a deep, spiritual truth that is intended to help us on our journey through life. The second commandment is intriguing, for God is recorded as saying, "You shall not make for yourself an idol in the form of anything in heaven above or on the earth beneath or in the waters below. You shall not bow down to them or worship them" (Exod. 20:4–5). An idol is something humans make of their own design to represent God. Idols have generally taken the form of a statue, which people would bow down to and worship as if the statue truly represented God.

In the second commandment, God says, "Please, whatever you do, don't do that. Don't use any kind of image that is going to reduce me to less than what I really am or that is going to distort who I really am. I don't want you to have a false image of me, because that would mean a false relationship with a false god."

A seeking friend of mine once expressed the frustration of many seekers when he asked, "Then why doesn't God make it clear? Why doesn't he just come down and make his existence conclusively known, letting everyone know exactly who he is and what he is like?"

My answer surprised him. "He did," I replied. "That is why Christians believe Jesus is so important."

WHY THE LIFE
OF JESUS MATTERS

Why are Christians intrigued by a lone historical figure from the distant past? This question is particularly pressing when you consider that his life doesn't come close to the world's definition of greatness.

Jesus was born in a small, obscure village, the child of a peasant woman. He didn't go to high school or college. He never traveled more than two hundred miles from the place where he was born. He never wrote a book. He never held an office. He was only thirty-three years old when the tide of public opinion turned against him, prompting even his closest friends to abandon him. He was turned over to his enemies and was nailed to a wooden cross to be crucified between two criminals. While he was dying, his executioners gambled for his clothing, the only property he possessed on earth. After he died, his body was placed in a borrowed grave through the pity of an acquaintance. Yet almost two thousand years have come and gone, and Jesus arguably remains the most important figure of the entire human race. Why? Let's begin with a closer look at his life, which countless numbers have found to be filled with far more significance than might appear at first glance.[1]

His Life Matters Because of Who He Was

Christians believe that Jesus was God in human form. This is not simply how Christians have chosen to interpret his life. Jesus himself made this claim.[2] Consider this section from the Bible in which Jesus spoke directly to the issue of his identity:

> The Jews [said to Jesus], "Aren't we right in saying that you are a Samaritan and demon-possessed?"
>
> "I am not possessed by a demon," said Jesus, "but . . . I tell you the truth, if anyone keeps my word, he will never see death."
>
> At this the Jews exclaimed, "Now we know that you are demon-possessed! Abraham died and so did the prophets, yet you say that if anyone keeps your word, he will never taste death. Are you greater than our father Abraham? He died, and so did the prophets. Who do you think you are?"
>
> Jesus replied, . . . "Your father Abraham rejoiced at the thought of seeing my day; he saw it and was glad."
>
> "You are not yet fifty years old," the Jews said to him, "and you have seen Abraham!"
>
> "I tell you the truth," Jesus answered, "before Abraham was born, I am!" At this, they picked up stones to stone him.
>
> John 8:48–59

Who is Jesus Christ? He referred to himself as "I AM." What an odd reply! Jesus was either using poor grammar, or he was trying to say something significant. Insight is found in the Old Testament Book of Exodus in which we find the story of Moses and the burning bush. God was speaking to Moses, telling him to go to the highest authority in Egypt—the Pharaoh—to demand that he release all the Hebrew slaves. Moses asked God to give him his name—the very name of God—so that he could tell the people exactly who had sent him. The answer God gave to Moses is found in Exodus 3:14: "God said to Moses, 'I AM WHO I AM. This is what you are to say to the Israelites: I AM has sent me to you.'"

And that phrase—I AM—came to be the most holy one in existence to the Jewish people because it was the very name of God. It was so revered that the Jews would not even write it out completely. They wrote only the consonants: YHWH. Now look again at what Jesus said about his identity: "'I tell you the truth,'

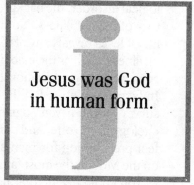

Jesus was God in human form.

Jesus answered, 'before Abraham was born, I am!'" (John 8:58).

Jesus claimed the name of God for himself. He said, "You want to know who I am? I'll tell you. I am God." And the people listening understood Jesus perfectly. They picked up stones to stone him. In their eyes, this was nothing less than blasphemy, for here was a mere man claiming to be God. Yet Jesus made this claim repeatedly throughout his life:

I am the Son of God.

John 10:36 TLB

I am the way, the truth, and the life.

John 14:6 GNB

The high priest asked him, "Are you the Christ, the Son of the Blessed One?" "I am," said Jesus.

Mark 14:61–62

Anyone who has seen me has seen the Father.

John 14:9

As a seeker, you must decide how you will interpret Jesus' claim. You could conclude that Jesus was a stark, raving lunatic. Maybe he did think he was God, but he had severe psychological problems. Yet in most cases of severe psychological disorder, the background of the person points to a history of mental illness. Nothing in the historical record of the life of Jesus reveals any of the classical manifestations of mental illness, such as the inability to relate to the real world, inadequacy in personal relationships, or deficiencies in verbal skills. In fact, psychiatrist J. T. Fisher concluded that if you were to survey all the psychological data that the discipline of psychology has to offer and boil it down to one essential and perfect prescription for mental health, it would be the Sermon on the Mount, the most famous sermon Jesus ever preached.[3]

You could decide that Jesus was simply a liar. He said he was God but knew he wasn't. This would mean, however, that the man whose teaching has set the standard for integrity and honesty throughout the civilized world was a habitual, pathological liar. Even more important to remember is that Jesus was arrested, mocked, beaten, and tortured prior to his execution. Jesus was offered a full pardon by the Roman governor, Pilate, if he would simply deny that he was God. If a con man could stop a nail from being driven into the flesh of his hand by telling the truth, he would. Such people only tell lies until their deception costs them more than what they might gain. But Jesus endured it all. He never denied his claim to be God, though given every chance.

A third option would be to say that Jesus was just a good man, maybe even a prophet from God, but that's all. Few want to say that Jesus was a liar or a lunatic, but they don't want to say he was God either. C. S. Lewis was a brilliant intellect who served as a professor at both Cambridge and Oxford. His comments on this option are worth reading:

I am trying here to prevent anyone saying the really foolish thing that people often say about Him: "I'm ready to accept

Jesus as a great moral teacher, but I don't accept His claim to be God." That is the one thing we must not say. A man who was merely a man and said the sort of things Jesus said would not be a great moral teacher. He would either be a lunatic—on a level with the man who says he is a poached egg—or else he would be the Devil of Hell. You must make your choice. Either this man was, and is, the Son of God: or else a madman or something worse. You can shut Him up for a fool, you can spit at Him and kill Him as a demon; or you can fall at His feet and call Him Lord and God. But let us not come with any patronising nonsense about His being a great human teacher. He has not left that open to us. He did not intend to.[4]

Because of his claim, Jesus was either something very much more than a great moral teacher, or something very much less. Christians believe that Jesus was who he said he was: God in human form.[5]

His Life Matters Because of How He Lived

Christians also believe the life of Jesus matters because, as God in human form, he lived a perfect life and gave us the best picture of how life ought to be lived. This is important because, without something to compare ourselves to, we have no idea whether our lives are being lived the way they were meant to be lived. Philip Yancey notes that the life of Jesus exposes us as human beings. We tend to look at our many faults and say, "That's just human." A man gets drunk, a woman has an affair, a child tortures an animal, a nation goes to war—that's just the human life. Jesus put a stop to such talk. By exemplifying what we ought to be like, he showed who we were meant to be and how far we miss the mark.[6] As Jesus himself said,

Are you tired? Worn out? Burned out on religion? Come to me. Get away with me and you'll recover your life. I'll show you how to take a real rest. Walk with me and work with me—

watch how I do it. Learn the unforced rhythms of grace. I
won't lay anything heavy or ill-fitting on you. Keep company
with me and you'll learn to live freely and lightly.

                                        Matthew 11:28–30 TM

His Life Matters Because of What He Taught

Finally, Christians believe the life of Jesus matters because
of what he taught. Mark, one of the four biographers of Jesus,
made an interesting observation about the life of Jesus, noting that, "The people were amazed at his teaching, because
[Jesus] taught them as one who had authority" (Mark 1:22).
Christians sense within the teachings of Jesus an authority
that isn't found anywhere else. Through his teaching, people experience an encounter with truth, something that can
be trusted. Jesus once said, "These words I speak to you are
not incidental additions to your life. . . . They are foundational words, words to build a life on" (Matt. 7:24 TM).

But what should someone make of a life that ended so
tragically? If the life of Jesus matters, is there significance to
his death as well? For a spiritual seeker, the Christian response is intriguing.

WHY THE DEATH
OF JESUS MATTERS

Christians are well known for making an intriguing claim: "Jesus died for you." If you're like many seekers, you wonder why Jesus had to die and why he had to die for you. To get a handle on this, we have to talk about the "s" word: sin. The significance of the death of Jesus will never make sense to you unless you understand the meaning of this word.

The "S" Word

The word *sin* comes from a Greek word that means "to miss the mark." When someone would shoot an arrow toward a target and miss, it was called a sin. It didn't matter whether the archer missed by an inch or by a mile, it was still a sin.

In the Bible we read, "All have sinned; all fall short of God's glorious ideal" (Rom. 3:23 TLB). The Bible teaches that when it comes to living life the way God intended, all people are "missers of the mark." It doesn't matter whether we miss by an inch or by a mile, no one hits the bull's-eye every time. A sin isn't just a failure to be perfect either. Sin speaks of willful choices and conscious decisions to disobey God. Sin is not merely a side effect of humanity; it is the choice we make with our very souls to go against the moral law and will of God.

Sin is serious business. The Bible contends, "The wages of sin is death" (Rom. 6:23). We are familiar with the reality of physical death, but the Bible also teaches the reality of spiritual death, which is separation from God. Sin causes spiritual death. It breaks our relationship with God and destroys the intimacy that God intended to take place between himself and his creation, because at its heart, sin is rebellion against God and his character. As a result, our sin separates us from God, and unless addressed, the separation remains.

His Death Matters Because He Took Our Place

In biblical times, God decreed that the payment for wrongdoing—for a sin—was through the blood of an animal. Though humanity's rebellion deserved death, God's love allowed for sin to be addressed through the sacrifice of an animal. That seems strange to us, but it was very intentional to God. He wanted people to see the severity of their sin. He wanted people to see that paying for their sin took an act that was messy, gruesome, and costly, because sin is messy, gruesome, and costly.

God also said that the animals sacrificed were to be without blemish or mark. The point was that sin, or imperfection, could only be made right by perfection. Then, at a point and time in history that God chose for reasons known only to him, God provided a perfect, once-and-for-all sacrifice for the sins of all people throughout all time and history. He offered the flawless, perfect life of his Son, Jesus, on the cross.

Jesus was the fulfillment of the sacrificial system, and because of him, we can now be forgiven once and for all. There doesn't need to be the continual sacrifice of animals because "unlike the other high priests, [Christ] does not need to offer sacrifices day after day, first for his own sins, and then for the sins of the people. He sacrificed for their sins once for all when he offered himself" (Heb. 7:27). Christians believe the death of Jesus matters because he took our place. Jesus loved each one of us so much that he gave his life for ours.[1]

Imagine you were driving your car, exceeding the speed limit, and you hit a child on her way home from school. You are brought to trial, and the judge turns out to be the child's father! The evidence is presented, and from his bench, the judge, barely controlling his emotions, states, "I find you guilty, and sentence you to death." But then he does a strange thing. With compassion in his eyes, he gets up from his bench, takes off his robe, walks down to where you stand, embraces you, and says, "But I love you. The penalty must be carried out, for I am an honest and good judge, and what you did was wrong. But I love you and do not want to see your life end this way, so I will go in your place." This is what Jesus did for us, and the wonder of it was not lost on the biblical writers:

> We can understand someone dying for a person worth dying for, and we can understand how someone good and noble could inspire us to selfless sacrifice. But God put his love on the line for us by offering his Son in sacrificial death while we were of no use whatever to him.
>
> Romans 5:7–8 TM

His Death Matters Because It Can Restore Our Relationship with God

Christians believe the death of Jesus matters not simply because he took our place and dealt with our sin, but because through his act, our relationship with God can be restored and spiritual death can be avoided. C. S. Lewis described this allegorically in his classic tale for children, *The Lion, the Witch and the Wardrobe.* Aslan the lion tells Susan and Lucy that "when a willing victim who had committed no treachery was killed in a traitor's stead, . . . Death itself would start working backwards."[2]

I once read about a little girl at the Stanford Medical Hospital who was suffering from a rare and serious disease. The doctors said she had one and only one chance at surviving— a complete blood transfusion. Not just any blood transfusion would work, however. The blood had to come from her five-year-old brother. Her little brother had somehow survived the same disease and had developed the necessary antibodies to fight off the illness. His blood was her only chance of survival. The family knew the little boy couldn't possibly understand all that was going on, much less why, so the doctor simply asked him if he would be willing to help his big sister by giving her his blood. The little boy looked at the doctor, looked at his sister, and then he said, "All right, I will. I'll do it if it will help my sister."

> Christ's death on our behalf— if accepted—is what bridges the gap between us and God that was created by our sin.

So they set up the transfusion. The little boy smiled at his sister as he saw his blood pass from his arm into hers. Then he looked up at the doctor, and with a trembling voice asked, "Will I start to die right away, or will it take a while?" Only then did they realize the boy thought it was *all* of his blood he had to give, and that it was his very life he was giving to his sister. As the sacrificial love of this young boy saved the life of his sister, so the sacrificial love of God through Christ saves us.[3]

Christ's death on our behalf—if accepted—is what bridges the gap between us and God that was created by our sin. As the apostle Paul wrote, "God is on one side and all the people are on the other side, and Christ Jesus . . . is between them to bring them together, by giving his life for all mankind" (1 Tim. 2:5 TLB).

This idea of a bridge is significant and is perhaps best grasped visually.[4] It starts with the realization that God wants to be in relationship with us; we matter deeply to him because he made us and loves us.

But we rebelled against God and disobeyed him. Our rebellion has separated us from God and broken off the relationship.

There are many ways we can try to get back to God, to restore the relationship, to bridge the gap. We can try good deeds, church attendance, obeying God's law, but each of these means falls short of bridging the distance. According to the Bible, none of these can wipe away our sins and repair our broken relationship with God. And as mentioned before, the penalty for our sin is death.

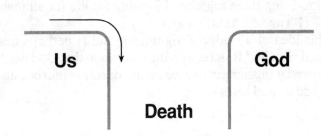

Yet in his love, God provided a bridge over which we can find forgiveness and the full restoration of our relationship with him. That bridge is the cross of Christ, on which Christ paid the penalty for our sin in full.

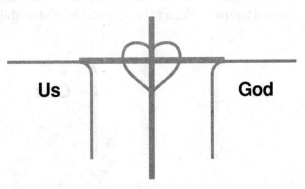

But just knowing about the cross and what it can do for our lives is not enough; the Bible teaches that we must act on this knowledge, that we must cross over to the other side.

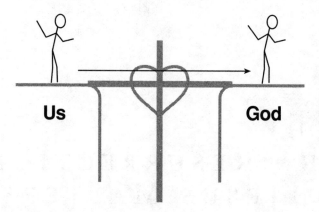

This is done by simply confessing our sin and acknowledging our need for God's forgiveness and leadership.

The cross matters to Christians because it is the bridge to a relationship with God.

WHY THE RESURRECTION OF JESUS MATTERS

As important as the life and death of Jesus are to Christians, these events mean nothing without the historical event that brought them to completion: the resurrection. On Easter Christians celebrate Jesus' resurrection from the dead, an event that makes it possible for people to trust in who Jesus was, experience a new beginning, receive power for living, and look to the future with hope.

His Resurrection Matters Because It Allows Us to Trust in Him

As mentioned before, Jesus claimed to be God in human form. If he was, the resurrection would obviously validate that claim. If he wasn't, his body would still be rotting in a tomb. The resurrection cuts to the heart of whether Jesus was who he said he was. Jesus himself set up this litmus test. Matthew, who wrote one of the four eyewitness accounts of Jesus' life, recorded what Jesus said:

As Jesus was on the way to Jerusalem, he took the twelve disciples aside, and talked to them about what would happen to him when they arrived. "I will be betrayed to the chief priests and other Jewish leaders, and they will condemn me to die. And they will hand me over to the Roman government, and I will be mocked and crucified, and the third day I will rise to life again."

Matthew 20:17–19 TLB

Jesus was, in fact, killed by the Roman authorities and placed in a tomb that was sealed and then guarded by Roman soldiers. On the third day after his death, the tomb was found empty. Jesus' followers announced that he had risen from the dead, and along with hundreds of others, claimed that they had seen him.[1]

Some might contend that the disciples stole the body of Jesus and then spread rumors about his resurrection. Jesus had said he would rise from the dead on the third day, so on the third day the disciples stole his body so it would look as if Jesus' claim had been fulfilled. According to this view, there were no postresurrection appearances and no empty tomb; the body was probably devoured by dogs, the fate most criminals crucified by the Romans suffered. Yet this fails to account for the amazing, overnight transformation of the disciples from a band of frightened cowards to a group of radical revolutionaries who willingly risked their lives to spread the message of the risen Jesus. Would they do this for a claim they knew to be a lie? A conspiracy theory must also account for the fact that, according to all four historical accounts recorded in the Bible, the first witnesses to the resurrection were women. Even the least sophisticated conspirators who wanted to authenticate a failed religious leader would not invent such a tale, for Jewish courts did not accept the testimony of female witnesses.

Even more telling is that all but one of the disciples who bore witness to the resurrection died the death of a martyr. John, the only exception, was exiled to the Island of Patmos, where he remained until his death.[2] Intriguingly, each of the disciples was faced with a moment of decision: Deny what you say about Jesus and his resurrection and live, or cling to your story and die a cruel death. The disciples never wavered in their commitment to the truth of the resurrection story. People will die for what they believe to be true, even though it may be false, but people do not die for what they know is a lie.[3]

Perhaps the Jewish or Roman authorities stole the body. This, however, raises a significant question: Why? The Roman authorities were the ones who put guards at the tomb to make sure the body *wasn't* stolen, understanding Jesus to be an incredible threat to both Jewish authority and Roman rule, and wanting desperately to ensure that Jesus' resurrection predictions could not be falsified by means of a stolen corpse. If they could have stopped the spread of Christianity by producing the body, they would have paraded it through the streets of Jerusalem, saying, "See, he was just a man— dead forever." They didn't.

This is also why few have theorized that the disciples went to the wrong tomb (the location of which was well known to everyone), or that it wasn't really Jesus on the cross. Both scenarios could have been cleared up if the Romans would have produced a body. This is also why you can't write off the resurrection and eyewitness accounts as some kind of mass hallucination due to overwhelming grief and emotional stress. Not only would a hallucination have to account for every eyewitness account—twelve postresurrection appearances are recorded in the New Testament alone, including one to over five hundred people—but the simple production of a dead body would have brought everyone back to reality.

A third explanation has been called the "swoon" theory.[4] According to this theory, Jesus didn't really die on the cross. The soldiers mistakenly reported him dead, when, in actuality, he had just swooned, or passed out on the cross from exhaustion, pain, and loss of blood. This theory holds that after Jesus endured thirty-nine lashes from the Roman guards (forty lashes was considered a death penalty), was pierced in the head with thorns up to two inches long, dragged his heavy wooden cross to the top of the hill of Golgotha, was nailed to its arms, was stabbed in the side with a lance, was pronounced dead by Roman medical experts, was laid in a damp tomb in burial clothes and seventy-five pounds of burial spices, and went three days without food, water, or medical attention of any kind, that this half-dead Jesus rolled back a stone weighing thousands of pounds, overpowered a crack team of Rome's elite fighting troops, walked miles on pierced feet, and then presented himself in such a strong and convincing manner that his once-frightened followers proclaimed him triumphant King over the grave.

As you might imagine, few have embraced this idea. Beyond the practical difficulties of such a theory, medical experts have come to the conclusion, based on the biblical record of Jesus' death, that he was in fact dead. According to the Book of Luke, when the spear pierced Jesus' side, water and blood spilled out. While of little significance to those who recorded this observation, medical analysts now see this as a description of the postmortem separation of the blood into clot and serum, indicating that Jesus was truly dead.[5]

So if the disciples didn't steal the body, the Jewish and Roman authorities didn't steal the body, the witnesses didn't go to the wrong tomb, Jesus didn't just pass out on the cross, and it really was Jesus who was crucified, what option is left? Christians believe Jesus did what he said he would do: He rose from the dead. So overwhelming was this evidence to the mind of one seeker, orthodox Jewish rabbi and scholar Pinchas Lapide, that he came to believe in the resurrection based on the historical evidence alone.[6] You might be saying, "This is just too incredible to believe. People don't come back from the dead." But if Jesus was who he said he was, God in human form, is it really so incredible?[7] If Jesus was

God in human form, it would have been *more* incredible for death to have had a hold on him.[8]

His Resurrection Matters
Because It Provides a New Beginning

For Christians, trust in the identity of Jesus is only the beginning of the relevance of the resurrection. It also offers us a chance for a new beginning.

Billy Crystal starred in the comedy *City Slickers,* a movie that exposed the midlife crisis of three men who were in search of themselves and their places in life. At one point in the movie, Mitch, the character played by Billy Crystal, turns to his boss and says, "Have you ever reached a point in your life where you say to yourself, 'This is the best I'm ever gonna look, this is the best I'm ever gonna feel, this is the best I'm ever gonna do,' and it ain't that great?" Later in the movie, his friend makes a similar assessment when he says, "At this point in life, where you are is where you are."

The whole point of the resurrection is that God can resurrect your life too! God can take your life, and no matter where you are or where you've been, he can give you a new beginning. The Bible says, "Just as Christ was raised from the dead . . . we too may live a new life" (Rom. 6:4). God wants to take your past mistakes, your past failures, even your past sins, and give you a new beginning.

His Resurrection Matters
Because It Provides Power for Living

In addition to a new life, Christians believe the resurrection of Jesus can give us the power we need to live the way God wants us to live. We live in a day of self-help books, seminars, and retreats. Such resources and experiences are useful for telling us what we are supposed to do, but they can't give us the power to do it! The Bible promises an external power source, claiming that the power to change our lives can come to us from God. We don't have it within us to live the way we want to live, much less the way we are supposed to live. But the Bible says that the very same power that raised Jesus from the dead is available for our lives: "How incredibly great his power is to help those who believe him. It is that same mighty power that raised Christ from the dead" (Eph. 1:19–20 TLB).

Millions of Christians can testify to the fact that God's power has altered their lives: Marriages that seemed beyond hope have been restored, long, habitual, destructive patterns of behavior have been broken, finances have been straightened out, difficulties on the job have been overcome, parenting challenges have been met. The resurrection of Jesus matters because it provides the power to change your life.

His Resurrection Matters
Because It Offers Hope for the Future

In a letter to a group of Christians who had just chosen to put their trust in Jesus, the apostle Paul reminded them of one more dynamic of the resurrection:

> If all we get out of Christ is a little inspiration for a few short years, we're a pretty sorry lot. But the truth is that Christ *has* been raised up, the first in a long legacy of those who are going to leave the cemeteries.
>
> 1 Corinthians 15:19–20 TM

The Bible says that if there was no resurrection, then there's no hope for life after death. If that's true, life has no purpose and no meaning. Søren Kierkegaard once compared such a view to a smooth, flat stone that is thrown over the surface of a pond. The stone dances and skims over the surface of the water until that moment comes when, like life without hope beyond death, it runs out of momentum and sinks into nothingness. In a similar vein, Samuel Beckett once wrote a play titled *Breath*. The curtain opens to a stage littered with garbage. A soundtrack plays, starting with a baby's first cry and ending with an old man's last, dying gasp. Then the curtain closes. Beckett's point is clear: Life is absurd, man is meaningless, existence is pointless. But Christians maintain that the resurrection *did* happen, and the Bible says that "because Jesus was raised from the dead, we've been given a brand-new life and have everything to live for, including a future in heaven" (1 Peter 1:3 TM). That means hope.

A young boy named Jeremy was born with a twisted body and a slow mind. At the age of twelve he was still in the second grade. He needed to be in a special school, but there weren't any nearby. Because he was diagnosed as terminally ill and seemed relatively happy in the regular school program, he was allowed to continue. Spring came, and all the children were talking excitedly about the coming of Easter. To teach the idea of new life and the coming of spring, Jeremy's teacher gave each of the students a plastic egg.

> "Because Jesus was raised from the dead, we've been given a brand-new life and have everything to live for, including a future in heaven" (1 Peter 1:3 TM).

She said, "Now I want you to take this home and bring it back tomorrow with something inside that shows new life. Do you understand?"

"Yes, Miss Miller!" the children responded—that is, all the children except Jeremy. He didn't say a word. He just stared at the teacher, then stared at his egg.

The next morning, all nineteen children came to school, laughing and talking as they placed their eggs in the large basket on top of Miss Miller's desk. When their math lesson was over, it was time to open the eggs. In the first egg, the teacher found a flower.

She said, "Oh, good! A flower is certainly a sign of new life! When plants peek through the ground, we know that the new life of spring is here."

A small girl in the front row waved her arm. "That's my egg, Miss Miller!" Then the teacher opened the other eggs. She found butterflies, a rock with moss on it, and several other objects that represented new life to those young minds. Then the teacher opened an egg that was empty. She knew it was Jeremy's, but she didn't want to embarrass him. She quickly placed the egg to the side and went on opening the others.

Suddenly Jeremy said, "Miss Miller, aren't you going to talk about my egg?"

Flustered, she said, "But Jeremy, your egg was empty."

He looked into her eyes and said softly, "Yes, but Jesus' tomb was empty too."

Then his teacher said, "Jeremy, do you know why the tomb was empty?"

"Oh yes, Miss Miller, I know why. Jesus was killed and put in there. Then his Father raised him up!"

Then the recess bell rang. As the children all ran out to play, Miss Miller sat at her desk and wept. Three months later, Jeremy died. Those who paid their respects at the mortuary saw an interesting sight: nineteen plastic eggs laid on top of his casket, all of them empty.[9]

THE BIBLE

As I write this, one of the most success-ful authors in America, John Grisham, has just written a new book. Upon its release, it immediately jumped to number one on the best-seller list. I have read all of Grisham's books and have enjoyed each one. They are page-turners, keeping you on the edge of your seat wondering what is going to happen next. As pop-ular as Grisham's books are, however, they are nothing compared to the best-selling book of all time, which is actually a collection of sixty-six books in one volume that was written by over forty authors over a period of several hundred years. To date, it has been translated into at least 1,200 languages, and between thirty and fifty million copies are sold each year. It's the Bible.

What Makes the Bible So Special?

The Bible has been revered by millions for centuries and is the most influential book ever written. What makes the Bible so special and so integral to the Christian faith?

It Was Endorsed by Jesus

The Bible is special to Christians because Jesus endorsed it. Today, endorsements written by famous people or experts

in a particular field are often placed on a book jacket to bol-
ster the book's credibility. The credibility of well-known people is used to establish the book's credibility. For a Christian,
there is no historical figure more credible than Jesus, and he
threw his entire weight behind the Bible.[1]

During Jesus' time, he accepted what we now call the Old
Testament as holy Scripture from God. This body of writing
is the foundation for each of the three largest religions in the
world, each of which holds to belief in one God: Judaism,
Christianity, and Islam. Jesus unqualifiedly endorsed its special nature: "I tell you the truth, until heaven and earth disappear, not the smallest letter, not the least stroke of a pen,
will by any means disappear from the Law [of Moses] until
everything is accomplished" (Matt. 5:18). He also said, "[The]
Scripture cannot be broken" (John 10:35). And in what may
be one of the most telling statements he made in regard to the
Old Testament, Jesus introduced a passage from the Old Testament Book of Psalms by saying, "David himself, speaking
by the Holy Spirit, declared . . ." (Mark 12:36). Clearly, to
Jesus the Old Testament was no ordinary book.

Jesus endorsed the New Testament by personally autho-
rizing its writers.[2] Jesus chose these men to speak in his name
and to carry his word to others. These men were handpicked,
commissioned, and authorized by Jesus for a ministry of
teaching what he had taught them. The truth they were to
communicate is what we call the New Testament. Because
the early Christians believed Jesus was God in human form,
they added the teachings of Jesus and his apostles to the Old
Testament as the Word of God. As a result, when the apostle Paul communicated the teachings of Jesus to the church
at Thessalonica, he praised them, saying, "When you received
the word of God, which you heard from us, you accepted it
not as the word of men, but as it actually is, the word of God"
(1 Thess. 2:13). This is why descriptions of the early church

note that "they [the church] devoted themselves to the apostles' teaching" (Acts 2:42).[3]

It Was Inspired

The second reason the Bible is awarded a special status by so many is due to its inspiration.[4] Sometimes we use the word *inspired* when we mean something was wonderfully creative, such as a painting by Rembrandt or a cantata by Bach. Sometimes we use the word to refer to how something affects us, such as a moving speech or a touching act. Inspiration, as it relates to the Bible, is much more profound. The apostle Paul declared, "All Scripture is God-breathed" (2 Tim. 3:16). "God-breathed" means that the writing is from God himself! Over three thousand times in the Bible we find the writers using some form of the expression "The Lord says." For example, the Bible records God saying to the prophet Jeremiah, "I have put my words in your mouth" (Jer. 1:9). The idea of inspiration is that God used people to write the books of the Bible, but he was so involved in the process that the writers wrote exactly what he wanted. One of the clearest expressions of this idea is found in the New Testament Book of 2 Peter:

> God used people to write the books of the Bible, but he was so involved in the process that the writers wrote exactly what he wanted.

> Above all, you must understand that no prophecy of Scripture came about by the prophet's own interpretation. For prophecy never had its origin in the will of man, but men spoke from God as they were carried along by the Holy Spirit.
> 2 Peter 1:20–21

It Claims to Be True

Finally, the Bible is special to Christians because it claims to be true. The Bible is not merely a collection of human opinions but a message that is foundationally true and trustworthy, literally God's word to us. As the apostle Paul explained in his second letter to Timothy:

> The whole Bible was given to us by inspiration from God and is useful to teach us what is true and to make us realize what is wrong in our lives; it straightens us out and helps us do what is right. It is God's way of making us well prepared at every point.
>
> 2 Timothy 3:16–17 TLB

This is why the word *revelation,* derived from the Latin word *revelatio,* which means "to draw back the curtain," is often used to describe the Bible. The Bible is God revealing himself and truth about himself that could not otherwise be known. The Bible gives guidance for virtually every area of life—work, marriage, family, relationships, finances, emotions, physical health—and millions have found it is guidance that works. People who have studied the Bible and faithfully applied its wisdom to their lives say that it has transformed their lives. They will tell you that biblical teachings have saved their marriages, helped them straighten out their finances, repaired their broken relationships, and revolutionized their attitudes toward work. Most importantly, they will tell you that the Bible has shown them how to have a relationship with God.

But Can I Believe It?

Should a seeker believe the Bible is special in these ways? While revered by many, there are also those who say the Bible is full of myths, riddled with contradictions, and marked by errors. As a result, it's both fair—and important—for a seeker to examine the Bible's credibility, beginning with the text itself.

The Bible's Textual Credibility

The Bible is an old book that has been copied thousands of times over a period of centuries. Is the text we have even reliable? Can we know what the authors of the Bible really wrote after all this time?

The integrity of any ancient writing is determined by the number of documented manuscripts or fragments of manuscripts we can examine. For example, there are only nine or ten good manuscripts of Caesar's *Gallic Wars* in existence, the oldest of which is a copy dating to nine hundred years after Caesar's time. Yet no historian of whom I am aware has serious doubts about the reality of Caesar or of the integrity of this text. Fewer than ten copies of the ancient manuscripts of Plato are available for study and comparison in order to determine the accuracy and quality of the transmission of his writings throughout the years. The oldest of these manuscripts is a copy dating to 1,400 years after it was originally written. Still, scholars do not discount the historicity of the writings of Plato or express concern that what remains of Plato's writings is less than true to his original thought.[5]

When it comes to the Bible, there are over five thousand handwritten manuscripts in the Greek language that support the writings of the New Testament. Many of the earliest copies are separated from the originals by only twenty-five to fifty years.[6] The text of the Old Testament is supported by such findings as the Dead Sea Scrolls discovered in 1947, which provided manuscripts one thousand years older than any previously known Hebrew manuscript of the Bible and represented every Old Testament book except Esther.[7] Simply put, the Bible is the most dependable ancient document in all of history in terms of textual credibility.

So why are there so many translations? Actually, it has little to do with the integrity of the text itself. The Old Testament was written in the language of its writers—Hebrew—and the New Testament was written in the language of its writers—Greek. The Bibles we read are translations of those languages into the English language. As with any translation from one language to another, some freedom often exists in regard to the most appropriate word or phrase that can be used to convey the idea behind the actual Greek or Hebrew word. New translations from trained linguists are always appearing in an effort to capture the original meaning of the Hebrew and Greek manuscripts in light of the ever changing dynamics of modern language.

The Bible's Historical Credibility

But simply because a *text* is sound doesn't mean that what it records is historically accurate. When the Bible says something happened, did it really happen? The text may have been preserved with integrity, but that doesn't mean what it says is true. As a result, the historical credibility of the Bible demands investigation.

Interestingly, many of the writers of the Bible invite such examination by claiming to be eyewitnesses to what they wrote or to have conducted such research themselves. For example, one of the four biographers of Jesus, a physician named Luke, writes the following at the start of his account:

> Many have undertaken to draw up an account of the things that have been fulfilled among us, just as they were handed down to us by those who from the first were eyewitnesses and servants of the word. Therefore, since I myself have carefully investigated everything from the beginning, it seemed good also to me to write an orderly account for you . . . so that you may know the certainty of the things you have been taught.
>
> Luke 1:1–4

And the apostle John wrote the following in one of his contributions to the New Testament: "That which was from the beginning, which we have heard, which we have seen with our eyes, which we have looked at and our hands have touched—this we proclaim concerning the Word of life" (1 John 1:1).

Merely claiming to convey factual historical truth as eyewitnesses, however, has little to do with whether the actual writings are true. How has the Bible stood up under outside examination? Consider the report of Sir William Ramsay of Oxford University. Regarded as one of the greatest archaeologists ever to have lived, Ramsay concluded upon his own examination that the writers of the Bible were historians of the first rank and should be placed alongside the greatest of historians. So overwhelming was the archaeological evidence in support of the truth of the Bible that Ramsay eventually became a Christian.[8] Dr. W. F. Albright, late professor emeritus of Johns Hopkins University, declared that there can be no doubt that archaeology has confirmed the historicity of the Bible.[9] Historian and archaeologist Joseph P. Free notes that recent discoveries have "produced material that confirm the Scriptures at point after point."[10]

For example, the Book of Genesis mentions the infamous cities of Sodom and Gomorrah, which were destroyed by God because of their inhabitants' utter abandon to wickedness. No record of such places existed outside the biblical record, leading many to question the Bible's historical credibility. Now, however, archaeologists have unearthed what looks to be the place of pagan worship for the inhabitants of the two cities at Bab ed-Dra, including evidence of sudden destruction about 2000 B.C.[11]

Even entire civilizations, such as that of the Hittites, were unknown outside the biblical record. Since a review of the known literature of the day revealed no mention of such a people, many historians concluded the Bible was simply in error. Then the capital city of the Hittite empire was discovered, as well as forty other cities that made up the empire.[12] Another example is King David. Although mentioned over one thousand times in the Bible, until recently, no record of such a person could be found outside the Bible. This led some to put the biblical King David on the same footing as the mythical King Arthur. Then in 1993 and 1994, at the northern Israelite site of Tel Dan, archaeologists found pieces of a three-thousand-year-old monumental basalt stone that bore inscriptions about the "King of the House of David."[13]

Not only have the Bible's claims been supported through archaeological evidence, but an archaeological discovery has never refuted a biblical claim. Renowned Jewish archaeological expert, Dr. Nelson Glueck, observed, "It may be stated categorically that no archaeological discovery has ever controverted a biblical reference."[14] In fact, so many archaeological discoveries have supported the Bible that Dr. John Warwick Montgomery, former dean of the Greenleaf Law School, noted that if you were to apply the Federal Rule of Evidence to the gospel records, "This rule would establish competency in any court of law."[15]

The historical integrity of the Bible also extends to include the Bible's record of such things as the teachings of Jesus. Some have conjectured that the Bible's record of what Jesus said and what Jesus *really* said are two different things. Yet recent evidence shows that biblical records such as the Gospel of Matthew are in fact firsthand, eyewitness accounts written as early as A.D. 50, rather than kernels of truth covered over time by layers of stories and traditions. This evidence counters the work of the Jesus Seminar, a group of fifty panelists who have sought media attention for their highly skeptical view of the historical reliability of the Gospels in regard to the life and teaching of Jesus.[16]

What of the Bible's record of supernatural events? It would be easy to dismiss such claims as false, and as a result, bring the entire Bible under a critical eye. But since the Bible has such historical credibility in terms of what archaeology can verify, it may be worth considering its validity in more remarkable areas as well.

Let's assume the events recorded in the Bible did not occur but were made up and recorded by the biblical writers. As a specific example, let's say the supernatural events surrounding the life of Jesus—recorded in the Bible as historical fact by eyewitnesses—were simply false. For the sake of argument, let's imagine Jesus never raised anyone from the dead, never fed multitudes with a few loaves of bread and some fish, and never healed anyone from even a headache. The New Testament was written within thirty years of Jesus' death.[17] This means that when the New Testament documents began to circulate, people were still alive who had lived during the time of Jesus. Further, the explosive growth of the Christian church suggests that these documents were widely circulated. If the remarkable, miraculous events recorded in the text hadn't occurred, the public would have laughed the early manuscripts right off the bookstore shelves.

For comparison, let's say I wrote a book about the 1997 NBA finals, only instead of saying Chicago beat Utah in six games, I said the Charlotte Hornets swept Utah in four games. Further, in my book I went into great detail about how the games were played, the spectacular performances of various players, how many points were scored, and that Glenn Rice was named Most Valuable Player.

We all know if I were to write such a book, even in the year 2027, no publisher would touch it, and even if they did, few readers would buy it. Why? Because it would still be known that Charlotte wasn't in the finals in 1997 and the Chicago Bulls defeated Utah. My account of what took place would be shouted down in the marketplace, ridiculed, laughed at, and rejected. I would be forced to recant and withdraw my work. No matter how well written, how passionately presented, it would not find a receptive audience. Too many people saw the games.

It is no different with the Bible. The New Testament documents were written and circulated in a short enough period of time that people who were alive at the time of Jesus were still around to either say, "Yes, that really happened" or "No, those guys are nuts!" And the writers of the New Testament were not laughed off the scene. Despite the fact that the manuscripts contained references to supernatural events and miracles that took place in public settings and that readers could have easily dismissed them if not factual, the New Testament documents—and the message they contained—spread like wildfire, beginning a movement of such proportions that the entire trajectory of human history was altered. Why? Because there were too many people who could say, "I was there, and it happened just as they said."

The Bible's Authoritative Credibility

Ultimately, every seeker must ask if the Bible is truly from God, if it has authoritative credibility as a spiritual text. How can a spiritual seeker determine the Bible's credibility in this regard? One area many have considered relates to prophecy. If the authors of the Bible foretold events with accuracy and were never wrong in their prophecies, it would be convincing evidence of the Bible's authoritative credibility for our spiritual lives. If such prophecies did not come true, or were—at best—average in their success rate, the Bible's position as an authoritative text would be dramatically weakened.

How does the Bible fare by such a test? Consider the prophecies surrounding the life and ministry of Jesus. In the Old Testament, almost eight hundred years prior to his birth, people prophesied that the Messiah would be born in a stable in Bethlehem, that he would be a descendant of David, that he would be betrayed for thirty pieces of silver, that he would be crucified, that his bones would remain unbroken, and that the soldiers would cast lots for his clothing. Sound familiar? If you know anything about the life and death of Jesus, these prophecies should, because every one of them came true.[18]

What is the likelihood that all of these prophecies, each one fulfilled in minute detail, came about—through chance—in the life and person of Jesus? This must be asked, because a questioning mind could simply say that the biblical prophecies in regard to the life of Jesus are just coincidence. Scientist and mathematician Dr. Peter Stoner, former chair of the department of mathematics and astronomy at Pasadena City College and later chair of the department of science at Westmont College, investigated this question with six hundred of his students. They sought to calculate the odds of just *one* biblical prophecy about the Messiah coming true in the life of Jesus the way it did. Eventually they determined that the odds of such an event were one in four hundred million. Stoner and his students then calculated the odds of eight of the prophecies made about the Messiah being fulfilled in Jesus' life by chance. The answer was one in ten to the seventeenth power—that's a figure with seventeen zeros behind it! Finally, Stoner examined the odds of forty-eight prophecies about the Messiah being fulfilled in the life and person of Jesus. His conclusion: one chance in ten to the 157th power.[19] Yet this is precisely what happened. But not just forty-eight prophecies came true. Three hundred and thirty-two distinct Old Testament prophecies concerning the Messiah were fulfilled in the life of Jesus.[20] For this to have happened by chance would be akin to a person randomly finding a predetermined atom among all the atoms in a trillion, trillion, trillion, trillion, billion universes the size of our universe.[21] For the seeker who is trying to determine whether to give authoritative credibility to the Bible, the odds that the Bible is the inspired Word of God are overwhelming based on prophecy alone.

The Bible's Internal Credibility

Finally, we must not ignore the Bible's internal credibility. One of the most common concerns about the Bible is that it supposedly contradicts itself. Other concerns that are often voiced include the idea that the Bible is full of errors in rela-

tion to what we know to be true about the world based on science, and that the Bible is obscure and difficult to understand.

Despite the number of authors and the span of time over
which it was written, the Bible is consistent in its message
from start to finish. You find the same view of God, the same
understanding of human nature, the same view of Jesus, and
the same understanding of God's plan on every page. In
regard to supposed contradictions and errors, the reality is
that they are seldom a result of the actual text of the Bible as
much as the wooden interpretation of the Bible that does vio-
lence to the author's intent.[22]

Like any other ancient document, the Bible must be read
in light of its culture, as well as the means of communication
writers used at the time of its composition. Even today we
speak of the sun "rising," never meaning to make a scientific
statement, for, of course, the sun does not "rise." To read
any document without considering a reasonable degree of
nuance is unfair to the text, which is why Christians contend
that no contradictions, no mistakes, no errors exist within
the Bible's pages that cannot be adequately explained.[23]

One must then consider the Bible's supposed obscurity in
terms of actual meaning. The heart of understanding the
Bible is simply to try to get at what the author meant. Most
of the time, this is the most obvious reading of the text. So
why do so many claim the Bible is difficult to understand?
For some, it is not a matter of grasping the most obvious
reading that causes problems but the acceptance of the implications of that reading.

Pretend your daughter and her boyfriend are going out
for a Coke on a school night. You say to her, "You must be
home before eleven." Now suppose it gets to be 10:45 and
the two of them are still having a great time. They don't want
the evening to end, so suddenly they begin to have difficulty
interpreting your instructions. They say, "What did he really
mean when he said, '*You* must be home before eleven'? Did
he literally mean us, or was he talking about you in a general

sense, like people in general? Was he saying, in effect, 'As a general rule, people must be home before eleven'? Or was he just making the observation, 'Generally, people are in their homes before eleven'? I mean, he wasn't very clear, was he?"

"And what did he mean by, 'You *must* be home before eleven'? Would a loving father be so adamant and inflexible? He probably means it as a suggestion. I know he loves me, so isn't it implicit that he wants me to have a good time? And if I am having fun, then he wouldn't want me to end the evening so soon."

"What did he mean by, 'You must be *home* before eleven'? He didn't specify *whose* home. It could be anybody's home. Maybe he meant it figuratively. Remember the old saying, 'Home is where the heart is'? My heart is right here, out having a Coke, so doesn't that mean I'm already home?"

"What did he really mean when he said, 'You must be home before *eleven*'? Did he mean that in an exact, literal sense? Besides, he never specified 11 P.M. or 11 A.M. And he wasn't really clear as to whether he was talking about Central Standard Time or Eastern Standard Time. I mean, it's still only quarter to seven in Honolulu. As a matter of fact, when you think about it, it's *always* before eleven. Whatever time it is, it's always before the next eleven. So with all of these ambiguities, we can't really be sure what he meant at all. If he can't make himself clearer, we certainly can't be held responsible."[24]

Without a doubt, some parts of the Bible are difficult to understand. It reflects the places, histories, cultures, and languages of places long ago and far away. Sometimes you need some background information on those issues to make sense of a passage, while other passages cause disagreement. On the essential teachings and issues, however, the Bible leaves little room for confusion. As Mark Twain quipped, "It's not the parts of the Bible I don't understand that disturb me, rather it's the parts of the Bible that I *do* understand that disturb me."

What *is* often confusing to people is the activity of God. It is to this topic that we now turn.

WHY IS THERE SO MUCH SUFFERING?

Christine Peters had come down from Ohio to visit her sister in South Carolina. At the end of her visit, she loaded her suitcase and a bag of peaches into her rental car, hugged her sister good-bye, and headed for the airport. It was July 2. She boarded the DC-9 at 6:10 P.M. for the forty-minute trip from Columbia to Charlotte, and from there she planned to go on to Pittsburgh.

But that isn't what happened. The flight she boarded was USAir flight 1016, the flight that at 6:42 P.M. crashed just outside the Charlotte-Douglas International Airport. Christine survived that night, but thirty-seven of the fifty-two passengers on board did not. Among those thirty-seven were parents with children, soldiers on leave, students and young professionals just beginning their careers. Rita and Steve Mattox were honeymooners, married just hours earlier. Denisha Holland was only nine months old. All dead.[1] If there really is such a thing as a loving God, there isn't a seeker alive who doesn't want to know why a tragedy such as this one is allowed to happen.

Even those who believe struggle. The daughter of Dallas and Sharon Davis, Kathy Lynn Seidl, was among the 168

killed in the bombing of the Alfred P. Murrah Federal Building in Oklahoma City. She was thirty-nine. In the two years
since the bombing, the couple has also lost their eldest daughter to lung cancer and their only son to an auto accident.
"I've asked the Lord no less than a thousand times, 'Why?'"
says Sharon Davis. "But the Lord isn't talking to me much
right now. I'm in the dark." Family friend Paul Heath ex-
presses the feeling of most: "It's not right."[2]

No answer can be given that will satisfy the emotional pain
of such suffering. In the movie *Shadowlands,* Anthony Hopkins portrayed British author C. S. Lewis, whose wife died
soon after their marriage. In the movie, a minister tries to give
Lewis a God-knows-best pat answer, causing Lewis to explode,
"No! This is a mess. That's all anyone can say—it's just a
mess!" But for most seekers, the search is not for an answer
that will alleviate the pain as much as for an explanation as to
why the pain was allowed in the first place. This is not a question that seekers must ask of the Christian faith alone. All religions must somehow try to speak to the reality of pain and suffering. But for those faiths that believe in the reality of a loving,
personal God who cares about his creation—such as Christianity—the question takes on an added dimension.

The Bible teaches that God is all-powerful, able to do anything he wants. Further, the Bible teaches that God is thor-
oughly good, not mean, capricious, or vindictive. Yet bad
things happen. There is suffering in the world. And for many,
many people, those dynamics just don't mix. If God is good
and all-powerful, he shouldn't let bad things happen. Since
they *do* happen, either God isn't good or he isn't all-powerful.
Rabbi Harold Kushner, in his book *When Bad Things Happen to Good People,* embraced the idea that God cares but is
powerless to do anything about it. Elie Wiesel said of the God
Kushner described, "If that's who God is, why doesn't he
resign and let someone more competent take his place?"[3]
This was the initial sentiment of C. S. Lewis, who wrote after
the death of his wife,

Not that I am (I think) in much danger of ceasing to believe in God. The real danger is of coming to believe such dreadful things about Him. The conclusion I dread is not, "So there's no God after all," but "So this is what God's really like. Deceive yourself no longer."[4]

Can God be redeemed from the pit of our pain? Is there an answer? Christians believe there is and that it lies within a thing called free will.[5]

The Reality of Free Will

The Bible teaches that God made us and loves us. That's why you and I are here. We were created to experience God's love and to enjoy a personal relationship with him. Because of this, God gave us the freedom to respond to that love or to reject it. This was essential to the relationship because love is meaningless unless it is freely given and freely received. For example, the love my wife has for me is meaningful because it is freely given; I don't force her to love me. If I did, there would be little value to her expression of love. The relationship between us would have no meaning. God could make us love him, but if he did, the relationship would be meaningless. The only way our relationship with God can hold any significance is for it to be freely chosen and freely entered. So when God made us, he gave us free will, which means we can choose to accept his offer of a love relationship, or we can reject it.

The Consequences of Free Will

According to the Bible, the first humans, Adam and Eve, made use of their free will when they chose to reject God's offer of a loving, intimate relationship by rejecting his leadership for their lives. They made the conscious, purposeful choice to disobey God and remove themselves from his authority. Through them, the world departed from God's rela-tional design. Each of us, like Adam and Eve, has used our free will in ways that have dishonored God and reflected rebel-lion and disobedience against God. Through such actions, we have distanced ourselves from God's offer of relationship.

All choices come with consequences. If they didn't, they wouldn't really be choices. The decision to reject God's lead-ership altered God's original design for how the world would operate and how life would be lived, ushering in sin and evil as well as the consequences of sin and evil. Theologians named this life-altering moment the fall and point out that we now live in a fallen world. In other words, we live in a world that has fallen from its original design. We live on a planet that is suffering from the choices we have made, choices that began with Adam and Eve, and choices we con-tinue to make to this day. The consequences of our choices run so deep that we face not only moral evil but natural evil as well. The whole world is sick—earthquakes, tidal waves, volcanoes, mudslides, fires, birth defects, AIDS, even mechanical failures on airplanes. As Philip Yancey has writ-ten in his book *Where Is God When It Hurts?*, our world is "The Stained Planet."[6] The very existence of suffering is a "scream to all of us that something is wrong . . . that the entire human condition is out of whack."[7]

This raises a provocative point: God is not the author of sin and suffering—*we* are. When children die of starvation, the question often is, "How could God allow such a thing?" The real question should be, "Why have *we* allowed it?" Though there is more than enough food, money, and re-sources available to alleviate famine worldwide, many of the more affluent countries keep these things to themselves and then make best-sellers out of books about dieting. The sim-ple fact is that God let us choose, and we did. We chose to reject God's management, and the consequences can be seen each time we turn on CNN. Even more pressing is what we do to ourselves. As psychologist James Dobson notes,

We drink too much, or gamble compulsively, or allow pornography to control our minds. We drive too fast and work like there's no tomorrow. We challenge the boss disrespectfully and then blow up when he strikes back. We spend money we don't have and can't possibly repay. We fuss and fight at home and create misery. . . . We toy with the dragon of infidelity. . . . Then when the "wages" of those sins and foolishness come due, we turn our shocked faces up to heaven and cry, "Why me, Lord?" In truth, we are suffering the natural consequences of dangerous behavior that is guaranteed to produce pain.[8]

Only if we were liberated from our collective choices and freed from the consequences of our history of decisions would pain and suffering leave the world. So why doesn't God do that? Because of the overwhelming good of free will.

The Good of Free Will

Even though it can be used in ways that reject his love and can have terrible consequences, God has determined that the gift of free will is worth it. Free will means we aren't mindless robots; we can think and choose for ourselves. If we turn to God, *we* have made the decision; we weren't forced to turn to him. This makes our relationship with God, as well as life itself, meaningful. As C. S. Lewis wrote in *The Problem of Pain*, "Try to exclude the possibility of suffering which the order of nature and the existence of free-will involves, and you will find that you have excluded life itself."[9] Could the God of Christianity step in and stop the consequences of our choices? Yes, but he doesn't, for to do so would violate our free will, and the violation of free will would end the possibility of true relationship between us and God. In spite of the suffering, in spite of the tragedies, in spite of the pain, freely choosing to accept or reject a relationship with God is of ultimate importance and carries eternal significance.

God has refused to let the perils of authentic love prevent him from loving. Those who blithely say, "If God had known that pain would come from creating beings with the freedom to choose, he should not have created them," know little of true love. As C. S. Lewis reminds us,

> To love at all is to be vulnerable. Love anything, and your heart will certainly be wrung and possibly be broken. If you want to make sure of keeping it intact, you must give your heart to not one, not even to an animal. Wrap it carefully round with hobbies and little luxuries; avoid all entanglements; lock it up safe in the casket or coffin of your selfishness. But in that casket—safe, dark, motionless, airless—it will change. It will not be broken; it will become unbreakable, impenetrable, irredeemable. . . . The only place outside Heaven where you can be perfectly safe from all the dangers . . . of love is Hell.[10]

Where Is God in the Suffering?

Where is God in the suffering? Where is God when you hurt? Does he care? According to the Christian faith, the answer is yes, a thousand times yes! He cares more than you can possibly imagine. And if you want to know where he is in regard to all the suffering that has come from people using their free will to reject him, the answer is he is right in the middle of it—hurting with people, suffering with people through the sickness, the tragedies, the disasters, the famines. He reaches out to each person, by name, in an effort to walk with them through their pain. This is why the Bible says, "The Lord is close to those whose hearts are breaking. . . . The good man does not escape all troubles—he has them too. But the Lord helps him in each and every one" (Ps. 34:18–19 TLB). Those who have opened up their heart to God's presence and comfort in the midst of their pain have found this to be true.

After being a prisoner in Ravensbruck, the infamous concentration camp of Nazi Germany, well-known Christian Corrie ten Boom traveled throughout the world, telling her story of suffering in the context of faith in God. For thirty-three years following Ravensbruck, she never had a permanent home. When she was eighty-five years old, some friends provided her with a lovely home in California. It was a luxury she never dreamed she would have. One day, as a friend was leaving her home, he said, "Corrie, hasn't God been good to give you this beautiful place?"

She replied firmly, "God was good when I was in Ravensbruck, too."[11]

One of the most difficult tasks I was ever called upon to perform took place when I was a pastor of a church outside Louisville, Kentucky, during my seminary years. A deacon in the church called me at home and told me the wife of his next-door neighbor had just committed suicide. She was the mother of five girls. Her youngest daughter had found her. He said, "Would you come?" When I arrived, I saw the five daughters and their father huddled in a corner of the house. I thought to myself, *What am I doing here? What could I possibly say? What can I do that would help at this moment?* I went over to the family, introduced myself, and said the only words I could think of: "I just want you to know that I'm sorry. I'm so very, very sorry."

The girl who had found her mother looked up at me and said, "Would you pray for us?" So I prayed. I don't remember a single word of that prayer, but when I finished, that little girl looked up at me and simply said, "God's here, isn't he?"

And I said, "Yes, he is."

She said, "I thought so. I could feel him hugging me when you prayed. It's going to be all right, isn't it?"

And I said, "Yes, honey, it's going to be hard, but it's going to be all right."

God cares about our suffering. He grieves over the ways free will is used to reject him. As one of my theology professors in seminary used to say, "It is the ulcer in God's own stomach." That's why he invests himself in the process of healing the wounds that have come from our choices, and he does this by entering into the suffering process with us in order to lift us out of it. You say, "Where? How? When?" And the answer is the cross. God in human form came to earth in the person of Jesus and suffered. He knows about pain. He knows about rejection. He knows about hunger, injustice, and cruelty—because he has experienced them all.

When Jesus was on the cross, God entered into the reality of human suffering, experiencing it just as we do, in order to demonstrate that even when free will was used to reject him, his love never ended. This was not suffering for its own sake, however, but suffering that would make it possible for us to use our free will and choose again! This time, the choice would be the right one. Becoming a Christian does not mean the removal of pain and suffering, but it does mean God will enter your life and give you his strength to help you through the suffering. Then, one day, you will be with him in heaven, where, the Bible says, "He will wipe away every tear from [our] eyes. There will be no more death or mourning or crying or pain. . . . Nothing impure will ever enter it" (Rev. 21:4, 27). The apostle Paul wrote about this as well:

> For all creation is waiting patiently and hopefully. . . . Thorns and thistles, sin, death, and decay—the things that overcame the world against its will at God's command—will all disappear, and the world around us will share in the glorious freedom from sin. . . . For we know that even the things of nature, like animals and plants, suffer in sickness and death as they await this great event. And even we Christians . . . groan to be released from pain and suffering. We, too, wait anxiously for that day when God will give us . . . bodies that will never be sick again and will never die.
>
> Romans 8:19–23 TLB

Recently, I was invited to a friend's house to have lunch with a special woman I have long admired from a distance: Joni Eareckson Tada. A tragic diving accident when she was a teenager left her a quadriplegic for life. When I walked into my friend's house, Joni was in the living room in her wheelchair being hand-fed because she doesn't have the use of her hands. She'll never be able to have children. She'll never walk, never be able to touch or feel with her hands, never be able to dress herself, comb her hair, or even embrace her husband. She's had to fight pressure sores from her wheelchair, weak shoulder muscles that come from holding up her head, back problems from having to sit in one position, and neck difficulties from constantly having to look up at people.

She dreams of being able to walk on a beach at sunset and feel the sand between her toes, of doing simple things such as brushing her teeth, cooking, cleaning, or making up a bed. But if I had to describe Joni, I would use words such as bright, cheerful, happy, joyful, bubbly, funny, and most importantly, content. She wasn't always that way, however. When her accident happened, she could not understand why God would allow such a thing to happen to her. She grew angry, bitter, and even contemplated suicide. She couldn't face the prospect of sitting down for the rest of her life without the use of her hands or her legs. All her hopes were dashed; her dreams gone. But over time, Joni began to develop a deeply personal relationship with God, one that surprised her with its depth, its meaning, and its fulfillment. She began to discover what she never knew before—joy. The joy came from discovering that she was a child of God and that being in a relationship with her heavenly Father through Christ was all she needed to be fulfilled.

Today, she is an internationally known mouth-artist, a talented vocalist, a radio host, an author of over seventeen books, and an advocate for disabled persons around the world. One of the organizations she leads collects old wheelchairs, cleans them up, pumps up the tires, tightens the

screws, replaces the old, worn-out parts, and then distrib-
utes them to underprivileged handicapped children in Third
World countries. Without Joni, these children would have to
crawl around in the dirt because they cannot afford crutches,
much less a wheelchair.[12]

Joni will tell you that life is good, that God has been good
to her, and that she is very, very content. Does she want to be
healed? Of course. Does she enjoy being in a wheelchair? No!
Does she resent God for giving her—and the rest of the
world—the free will that ultimately caused her handicap? Not
on your life. She knows God could wipe out all evil, all suffering this very night. But he doesn't, and the reason he doesn't
is because of his love for people like her—and for people like
you. After all, if at midnight tonight God decreed that all evil
be stamped out in the universe, how many of us would be here
at 12:01? This is why the Bible says, "The Lord . . . is patient
with you, not wanting anyone to perish, but everyone to come to
repentance" (2 Peter 3:9). God's hope is that your search process—the one he has allowed you to pursue with your own free
will—will result in an authentic relationship with him.

> **The real question is whether you, as a seeker, will allow the reality of pain and suffering to drive you *away* from God or *to* God.**

The real question, therefore, is whether you, as a seeker, will
allow the reality of pain and suf-
fering to drive you *away* from God or *to* God, where he can
wrap his arms around you and walk with you through the
darkest night toward the promise of a brighter tomorrow.
There will be many times when God doesn't make sense,
when the awful "why" rings in your ears without an appar-
ent answer. At such times, though you do not know the
answer to the question, you can trust God, who does know

why, and you can pray, "Father, I do not always understand you, but I do trust you and your love for me."[13]

James Dobson tells about a five-year-old boy he encountered while he was on the attending staff at Children's Hospital, Los Angeles. The boy was dying of lung cancer, a terrifying disease in which the lungs fill with fluid and the patient is unable to breathe. It is a frightening experience, especially for a small child. The little boy had a Christian mother who loved him and stayed by his side through his long ordeal. She cradled him on her lap and talked softly about Jesus.

A nurse on staff at the hospital entered the boy's room one day as the boy was nearing death. She heard the child talking about bells. Cradled on his mother's lap, the little boy said, "The bells are ringing, Mommy. I can hear them."

The nurse thought he was hallucinating because he was close to death. She came back a few moments later, though, and he was still talking about the ringing bells. The nurse looked at the mother and said, "I'm sure you know your boy is hearing things that aren't there. He is hallucinating because of the sickness."

The mother just pulled her son closer to her chest, smiled, and said, "No, miss. He is not hallucinating. I told him when he is frightened—when he can't breathe—if he listens carefully, he can hear the bells of heaven ringing for him. This is what he's been talking about all day."

Later that night that precious little boy died on his mother's lap. When the angels came and took him home, he was still talking about the bells of heaven, bells that were rung by God, just for him.[14]

THERE CAN'T BE ONLY ONE WAY

When I was a freshman in high school, I tried out for the varsity basketball team. On the first day of tryouts, the coach ran a scrimmage, periodically sending players into the game to see how they played. When my turn came, I intercepted a pass on the very first play. Then I took the ball the length of the court, skyed over every other player, and made the prettiest layup you ever saw.

The coach instantly blew the whistle, stopped the game, and called me over to the bench. I was walking ten feet off the ground. I just knew my shot was so good that he had to stop the game just to tell me. I envisioned that *ESPN* had called and wanted the footage, and that *Sports Illustrated* had every intention of running a photo of me on the next cover. The shoe deal with Nike was only a matter of time. So I walked—actually, strutted—to the sideline.

My coach said, "White, that was a great shot. Your form was great, your intensity was great. Only thing is, you went to the wrong basket—but it was a great shot!"

Is there a right and a wrong basket in the spiritual game? Is Christianity the only way to score with God or simply one of many ways? For today's spiritual seeker, this is hardly academic. The religious landscape of modern American society can be nothing less than bewildering. Malise Ruthven termed it the "divine supermarket."[1] Religious groups, sects, cults, movements, philosophies, and worldviews abound in incredible numbers and diversity. If you're looking for an authoritative spiritual text, you can choose the Bible, the Bhagavad Gita, the Koran, or the Book of Mormon. Religious leaders include the Pope, the Dalai Lama, Hare Krishna, Buddha, or Mohammed. When it comes to groups, you can join the Mormons, Jehovah's Witnesses, the New Age Movement, Muslims, Jews, Christians, or those that adhere to Scientology. Barrett's *World Christian Encyclopedia* lists over twenty thousand denominations, with over two thousand in the United States alone.

Add to this mix one of the most pervasive, fundamental convictions of contemporary American society: All roads lead to God, and to say that one way is right and all the other ways are wrong is narrow-minded, bigoted, and prejudicial. What is true for you is true for you, and what is true for me is true for me. Searching for God is like climbing a mountain. Since everyone knows there is not just one way to climb a mountain—mountains are too big for that—each person can choose from a number of paths. God is also too big to be thought of or worshiped in just one way. All the ideas about God contained in the various religions of the world are just different ways up the mountain. In fact, though different religions have different names for God, the names all refer to the same God.[2]

Why Many People Believe in More Than One Way

Is it true that lots of roads lead to heaven, which means we really don't have to worry about which road we're on? Is it true that no person, no religion, no group, no book has a handle on the truth? Is it true that all religions are basically the same and all religious leaders are essentially of one mind so that ultimately all spiritual pursuits lead to the same place? If so, seekers need not look for spiritual truth. They just need to decide on spiritual preference. The spiritual search becomes a walk down a celestial food bar. Seekers go down the line, see all that's there, and then put on their plates what they want. However, if all roads do not lead to God, those who seek have embarked on nothing less than a search that by its very nature is scandalously exclusive.

If you embrace the idea that multiple paths lead to God and you turn out to be wrong, the consequences are enormous. It is wise, therefore, to walk through the reasons as to why people hold to this belief to determine if such an idea is sound.

There Are So Many Religions

The sheer number of faiths from which to choose convinces some people that there is more than one path to God. Religious pluralism has existed for centuries, but never have people been exposed to so many faith options as we are today.[3] As the number of religious options increases in one's mind, the idea that one option represents ultimate spiritual truth lessens. Yet the mere presence of options has little to do with whether a particular faith might be true, nor with whether ultimate spiritual truth actually exists. The simple fact is that a test may be multiple-choice, but that does not mean it has multiple answers.

The Belief That All Religions Are Basically the Same

The idea that all paths are legitimate is also fueled by the sentiment that all religions are basically the same. Many introductory courses in world religions on the high school and college level stress the common denominators of religion throughout time and culture. The belief in a higher power, the existence of an afterlife, and the need for spiritual enlight-enment seem to bind all religious expression together. This can lead some to believe that the particular religious faith they select is not as important as striving for spiritual development in one fashion or another.

Yet while a course in world religions will reveal certain similarities between various world religions, it is also true that they contradict each other in crucial areas.[4] For example, Christians believe in God, while some Buddhists don't even teach that there is a God. Those who embrace Hinduism have no trouble with the idea of a deity. In fact, they claim that there are *many* gods. Christians, however, claim that there is one and only one God. Christians also embrace Jesus' claim that he was God in human form who came to restore our relationship to God. Muslims, on the other hand, don't believe that Jesus was God at all. Christians believe in truth and error, right and wrong, morality and immorality, while adherents to the various forms of New Age thinking contend that there are no absolutes and everything is relative. Even the nature of one's relationship to God differs radically from faith to faith. Compare the story of the prodigal son from the teaching of Jesus with a similar Buddhist narrative. In both, a boy comes home from his errant ways and is met by his father. While the boy in Jesus' story is met with undeserved forgiveness and love, his Buddhist counterpart has to work off the penalty for his past behavior through years of servitude.[5]

Somebody is right and somebody is wrong, or everyone is wrong, but you can't say that everybody believes about the same thing. That would be intellectually dishonest in light of the facts. If God exists—unless he is some senile, confused, muddled, schizophrenic, unbalanced being who isn't sure what he stands for—there *is* religious truth and religious falsehood among the competing views. And the areas of disagreement among those views are not trivial in nature. The nature of God, the identity of Jesus, and how we enter into a

relationship with God are of paramount importance. To return
to our mountain climbing analogy in which all paths lead to
the same peak, the truth is that there isn't a single peak, much
less a single idea of what the peak even looks like. Instead,
the mountain has many different peaks, which raises a very
significant question: How do you get to the highest one?[6]

The Idea That Sincerity Is What Matters

A third reason one might believe that many roads lead to
God is the feeling that all that really matters is one's sincerity. It isn't *what* a person believes that matters, but *how* he
or she believes it. Something deep inside of us knows, and I
think correctly, that the nature of true spirituality is somehow connected with authenticity. This is why a person such
as Mother Teresa, who was a Christian, was so widely re-
spected by Christians and non-Christians alike.

But it is one thing to value sincerity and another to make
sincerity the lone characteristic of spiritual truth. *How* you believe matters, but so does *what* you believe. If you say it doesn't
matter what you believe as long as you are sincere, you miss a
very important point: You can be sincerely *wrong*. If I have a
headache at three o'clock in the morning and I blindly reach into
my medicine cabinet, I can sin-
cerely believe I am taking an aspirin, but if I am really taking cyanide, my sincerity will not save me from the perils of
the poison I've ingested. If I put carbolic acid in my eyes
instead of contact lens solution, no matter how sincerely I
believe it is okay, I will still do damage to my vision. During

> If you say it doesn't matter what you believe as long as you are sincere, you miss a very important point: You can be sincerely *wrong*.

World War II, Adolf Hitler sincerely believed that the slaughter of six million Jews was justified—but he was sincerely wrong. Sincerity matters, but it cannot be all that matters, because sincerity alone cannot alter reality. Therefore, it is not simply the sincerity of our faith that matters but the *object* of our faith as well. Faith is very much like a rope. It matters what you tie it to.

The Belief That No Religious Group Should Think It Is Better Than Any Other

Some people are offended by religious groups that think their religion is better than any other religion. Because God is so big and our understanding is so small, it is nothing less than arrogance and narrow-mindedness for a single religious group to maintain that it holds all truth. To ensure that tolerance of other people's views exists, one should not claim some people are wrong and some people are right—or that "wrongness" or "rightness" even exist.

But let's imagine a young student who is given a question on a math test in school. The question is, "What is two plus two?" The answer, of course, is "four." But let's say the child answers "thirty-seven." Is the teacher intolerant, narrow-minded, and bigoted if she corrects his answer?[7] Or imagine a blind man is standing on the edge of a cliff and he turns to you and asks, "Which way should I step?" Would it be best for you to respond, "I really shouldn't say that one direction is better than another." Or imagine going to a doctor. Would you want to hear her say, "You have a malignant tumor spreading throughout your body. I think I know how to cure it, but to say so seems arrogant and I risk being narrow-minded in regard to other options. So I think it's best for me to say nothing at all."[8]

Everyone must avoid a spirit that persecutes people for their differing beliefs or denies them their religious freedom. But this spirit of tolerance is different from believing all points of view are equally valid. Just because you come to a conclusion about where you should place your spiritual trust does not mean you are intolerant of other beliefs. It does not even mean you deny that some truth can be found in other perspectives. As C. S. Lewis once observed, "If you are a Christian you do not have to believe that all the other religions are simply wrong all through. . . . If you are a Christian, you are free to think that all those religions, even the queerest ones, contain at least some hint of the truth."[9] Returning to our math student, there is one and only one *right* answer to "two plus two," but there are other answers that are much closer to being right than still others.

They Don't Believe in Truth

Ultimately, the question is whether people believe in truth, and today, many do not. A study by the Barna Research Group discovered that 66 percent of all Americans deny the existence of absolute truth.[10] As Allan Bloom has observed from his years teaching in a university classroom, there "is one thing a professor can be absolutely certain of. Almost every student entering the university believes, or says he believes, that truth is relative."[11] As a woman named Sheila described her faith to sociologist Robert Bellah, "I believe in God. I'm not a religious fanatic. I can't remember the last time I went to church. My faith has carried me a long way. It's Sheilaism. Just my own little voice."[12]

The most enduring and accepted definition of truth is the correspondence between our ideas or perceptions and reality.[13] If I make the statement "It is raining," it is true if I look outside and find that it is raining. What is true is that which actually *is*.[14] The belief in more than one way to God is really a belief that truth does not exist, or even more to the point, that it doesn't matter. Yet nowhere in life does this match our experience. For example, if you enter a phone booth, you cannot dial any set of numbers and get your home. Every residence and business has a separate number that must be dialed to reach that location. If you want to drive your car to Florida, you can't drive down any road that strikes your fancy, make any turn you want, get on any interstate that looks appealing, and arrive at your intended destination. If you have a headache, you cannot take any medicine you want and find relief. Some pills might help; others might kill. There is not a single area of life in which you can make any choice you want from a wide array of options and achieve the same result or experience. Today's spiritual seeker has to ask why an idea that fails when applied anywhere else in life is somehow true when it comes to the spiritual realm. Even a skeptic as noteworthy as Sigmund Freud maintained that if "it were really a matter of indifference what we believed, then we might just as well build our bridges of cardboard as of stone, or inject a tenth of a gramme of morphia into a patient instead of a hundredth, or take tear-gas as a narcotic instead of ether."[15]

The question, therefore, isn't "Is there truth?" (there is, and we live our lives by it every day) but "Can spiritual truth be found?"[16]

Christ's Outrageous Claim

Perhaps now the most incredible spiritual claim in all of human history can be heard. Jesus said: "I am the way and the truth and the life. No one comes to the Father except through me" (John 14:6). Not *a* way, *a* truth, or *a* life, but *the* way, *the* truth, and *the* life. It is this idea that marks the Christian faith. In the Book of Acts, we read the apostle Peter's proclamation: "It is by the name of Jesus Christ . . . Salvation is found in no one else, for there is no other name under heaven given to men by which we must be saved" (Acts 4:10, 12). While you may be initially shocked by this outrageous claim, you should not dismiss it simply because there are so many other religions and religious ideas. While there are many religions from which to choose, they differ radically from one another, and choosing where to place your spiritual trust is neither narrow-minded nor intolerant. Truth exists, and it matters. If all roads do not lead to God, then your spiritual search will lead you to the scandalous reality of one way. Christians believe that way is through a person—Jesus Christ.

But Even Christians Can't Agree!

Right about now, you may be asking a very fair question: "If Jesus is the one great truth of the spiritual world, why can't even Christians agree about what to believe?" You're in good company. In the Bible, we find that Jesus expressed this same concern: "I'm praying . . . for those who will believe in me because of them [the disciples] and their witness about me. The goal is for all of them to become one heart and mind" (John 17:20–21 TM). Jesus wanted his followers to be united through the basic doctrines of the Christian faith as he had taught them, as well as the spirit of authentic Christian community.

Sadly, division and discord exist among Christians concerning these very things. But it has been the exception to the rule. While some of the differences between Christian denominations are real, they are seldom substantive in regard to the basic doctrines of the Christian faith. Instead, they reflect preferred styles of worship, patterns of organization, approaches to ministry, and understandings of custom and tradition. Think of it in terms of clothing. Many of the differences among Christians are like the differences among people in the style of clothes they wear. They are all humans underneath, but their clothes display their different personalities and cultures.[17] It would be a mistake to assume that the many churches and denominations within Christendom reflect a state of division and chaos. There is instead a unified set of beliefs that has been coupled with great freedom and diversity in the expression of that faith.

What about Everyone Else?

If Christianity is the only way, does that mean God is going to send everyone else to hell? The Bible teaches that it isn't God's desire for anyone to experience hell as a punishment for his or her broken relationship with God. Rather, he desires for everyone to receive the gift of eternal life in heaven through Christ. But since God didn't make mindless robots, we have the ability to freely accept or reject that gift. Of course, with our freedom to choose comes consequences. If it didn't work this way, our choice would be meaningless. God doesn't send anyone to hell. We choose our own destination of our own free will.

Look at how the apostle John puts it: "Whoever believes in him [Jesus] is not condemned, but whoever does not believe stands condemned already because he has not believed. . . . This is the verdict: Light has come into the world, but men loved darkness instead" (John 3:18–19). For the person who has chosen to embrace the Christian faith, the judgment of God will simply affirm the decision that has already been made. Take a look at how Jesus phrased it: "I tell you the truth, whoever hears my word and believes him who sent me has eternal life and will not be condemned; he has crossed over from death to life" (John 5:24).

But what of the "good" people who, for whatever reason, do not choose to embrace Christianity? Are they as subject to the exclusive nature of spiritual truth as everyone else? Let's reflect on this idea of good. The Bible teaches that no one is truly good, and even our most noble spirits—from Gandhi to Mother Teresa—would agree. As Joseph de Maistre once observed, "I do not know what the heart of the rascal may be; I know what is in the heart of an honest man;

it is horrible."[18] No one is in less of a broken relationship with God and in need of the way to God than anyone else.

What about those who have never been exposed to the Christian faith, or the child who dies at a very early age, or the person who is mentally challenged? The Bible is clear in its affirmation that God's character is perfect, which means he is just. All people will be judged according to the knowledge they have and their ability to respond to that knowledge.[19] As C. S. Lewis remarked, "We do know that no man can be saved except through Christ; we do not know that only those who know him can be saved through Him."[20] This does not mean that people will be saved by Christ through the channel of other religions but simply that all persons will be judged fairly by God on the basis of their knowledge of Christ and their ability to respond to that knowledge. So while Christians believe that choices have consequences and hell is real, no one *has* to go there. *The* way, *the* truth, and *the* life are available to us all.

DISAPPOINTMENT WITH CHRISTIANS

Weddings are staged to be beautiful events. Robert Fulghum writes of one mother who had seven months to plan her daughter's wedding, and no detail was overlooked. Anything that could be engraved was engraved. She arranged teas and showers and dinners. An eighteen-piece brass and wind ensemble was hired for the occasion. The bride's wish list for home furnishings was registered in stores as far east as New York and as far south as Atlanta. Not only were the bridesmaids' outfits made to order, but the groom and his groomsmen *bought* their tuxedos. They didn't rent them, mind you, they *bought* them.

The wedding day finally arrived. Everything had been planned, and nothing had been left to chance. Guests in formal attire arrived and began to fill the church. Enough candles were lit to light up Manhattan. The orchestra played beautifully. The mother of the bride coasted down the aisle like a performer at an opera. You could see the look of satisfaction on her face. She had pulled off perfection, and everyone who was anyone to her was there to see it.

The nine bridesmaids entered, then the groom and his men took their places. The wedding march thundered, and in came the bride. Every head turned. Once the bride reached the front of the church, she looked to her left, looked to her right, and then promptly vomited all over her dress, her ring bearers, her flower girls, and perhaps most fittingly, all over her mother.[1]

Problems with Christians

A bride is traditionally clothed in a beautiful white gown symbolic of her spotless character, impeccable appearance, and perfect deportment. The nightmare is for any imperfection to break through the illusion. We know the bride is human, frail, and flawed, but the ceremony and her appearance invite us to see her as somehow above the imperfections of our race. If humanity does break through, it is shocking and dismaying. It is one thing to be imperfect in everyday life—it is an altogether different experience when one is dressed in white.

Professing Christians can be seen as brides dressed in white, seemingly inviting us to embrace the illusion of perfection. When imperfection breaks through, cynicism toward the Christian faith as a whole creeps in. And there is no shortage of imperfection.

Some Christians Are Immoral

In recent years, the media has confronted us with stories of ministers charged with molesting young children, church leaders who have embezzled funds from church accounts, and pastors caught in adulterous affairs. Scores of religious celebrities and leaders have been exposed for sexual or financial impropriety. Such behavior has been evident among Christians even from the earliest days of the movement. In the New Testament Book of 1 Corinthians, the apostle Paul wrote this to a church: "It is actually reported that there is sexual immorality among you. . . . Shouldn't you . . . [be] filled with grief?" (1 Cor. 5:1–2). The apostle Paul was shocked and disillusioned at the way certain Christians were behaving, just as people are shocked and disillusioned today.

Some Christians Are Inflexible

Christians can also be inflexible and rigid in their thinking, becoming pushy and narrow-minded, exhibiting a spirit of intolerance toward other perspectives. They remind us of the young boy scout who was asked by his scoutmaster if he had done his good deed for the day. The young boy honestly replied that he had not, so the scoutmaster told him to go out and not come back until it had been done. Twenty minutes later the little boy returned, his clothes in shreds, and his hair going in ten different directions. Even his face was cut and bleeding.

The scoutmaster said, "My goodness, son, what have you been doing?"

"I did my good deed for the day, sir," the boy said.

The scoutmaster said, "What did you do?"

"I helped an old lady across the street."

"Then why are you in this condition? Your clothes are torn, your hair is messed up, your face is cut and bleeding. What happened?" asked the man.

"Well," the boy said, "she didn't exactly want to go."

Jesus never intended for the people who followed him to act in such a way. In fact, irreligious people so enjoyed Jesus' company that they even invited him to their parties. While Jesus never compromised his convictions, beliefs, or teachings and taught openly about living a life that pleased God, those who heard him never doubted his sincere respect and love for them as persons.

Some Christians Are Strange

A third concern is that some Christians seem, well, a little strange. During college, before I chose to follow Christ, I thought the Christian organizations on campus were nothing more than groups of social misfits who couldn't get a life for themselves anywhere else, so they formed little Bible clubs where they could sit around and talk in King James English and once a month get radical and go on a hay ride. I thought they rejected all forms of contemporary music, didn't like sports, and had never been to a movie that wasn't put out by Disney. I had the idea that guys who were Christians buttoned their shirts to the very top, wore pants that were too short, had slide rule calculators strapped to their waists, and had about forty pens stuck in their pockets. Bottom line: These were not people I wanted to spend time with. When I actually attended a meeting of one such organization—InterVarsity Christian Fellowship—all my caricatures were blown away. I encountered normal people who dressed normally, talked normally, acted normally—yet were committed Christians!

While some people who call themselves Christians can seem to be out of synch with normal behavior, Christ doesn't call anyone to live a fringe existence. He called his followers to live for him in a way that was both winsome and compelling. When the Bible records the lifestyle of the early Christians, it says that they "devoted themselves to the apostles' teaching and to the fellowship, . . . and to prayer. . . . [and they were] enjoying the favor of all the people" (Acts 2:42, 47). The lifestyle they led was radically different from that of the people around them, but their personalities and lives were of a sort that drew people to them. They were different but never repulsive.

Some Christians Are Uptight

Many seekers encounter a number of seemingly uptight Christians—people who can't seem to loosen up, have a good time, and enjoy themselves. It's as if Christ functions as the cosmic killjoy in their lives. Rather than a spirit of joy, these people seem to exhibit a spirit of legalistic confinement. Yet the Bible says that "the Son of Man [Jesus] came, enjoying life" (Matt. 11:19 PHILLIPS). The Bible also informs us that Jesus enjoyed friends, played with children, went to numerous parties, and had a good sense of humor!

You say, "Wait a minute—Jesus told jokes?" Yes, he did. Jesus was a Hebrew. Every culture has its own sense of humor. The Hebrew form of humor was exaggeration. So when Jesus told the religious hypocrites to take the log out of their own eye before they worried about the speck in somebody else's, people cracked up![2] They said, "Hey, that's a good one, Jesus!"

There was nothing uptight about Jesus, and there's nothing necessarily uptight about the Christian life. In fact, Jesus said, "Keep company with me and you'll learn to live freely and lightly" (Matt. 11:30 TM). Some uptight people might be Christians, but Christianity didn't make them that way.

Some Christians Are Unloving

Many seekers also struggle with the number of Christians who appear to be unloving, even mean-spirited. The media has often captured sermons and protests, demonstrations and interviews in which some Christians seem to be at war with the world in a spirit of hatred. And it's not just toward non-Christians that Christians appear unloving. It doesn't seem as though some of them care that much about each other either! Churches fight and split, denominations argue and divide, and people with moral failures are dismissed with cold condemnation. Are Christians unloving? Sadly, many of them are. But the Bible doesn't support anything that's out of step with a demonstration of love, being very explicit in what that love should be like:

> Love is patient, love is kind. It does not envy, it does not boast, it is not proud. It is not rude, it is not self-seeking, it is not easily angered, it keeps no record of wrongs. Love does not delight in evil but rejoices with the truth. It always protects, always trusts, always hopes, always perseveres.
>
> 1 Corinthians 13:4–7

Some Christians Are Judgmental

It is not uncommon for a seeker to be turned off to the Christian faith because of the judgmental attitude of a particular Christian. It's as if they feel the Christian says, "What you are doing is wrong. Let *me* tell you how to live your life!" Even further, some Christians base their approval of others on where they stand on certain social or political issues.

While Jesus called his followers to a moral life and to have the courage and willingness to take a stand for truth in the cultural marketplace, he strongly condemned a judgmental attitude born of spiritual pride. Read his words for yourself:

> Do not judge. . . . Why do you look at the speck of sawdust in your brother's eye and pay no attention to the plank in your own eye? How can you say to your brother, "Let me take the speck out of your eye," when all the time there is a plank in your own eye? You hypocrite, first take the plank out of your own eye.
>
> Matthew 7:1, 3–5

Some Christians Are Hypocritical

Finally, some seekers think a great many Christians are hypocritical. The word *hypocrite* is taken from a Greek word that refers to the wearing of a mask. In ancient Greece, actors often wore masks corresponding to the characters they played. A character's role was a facade, an "act." Hypocrites, then, are mask wearers. They appear to be one thing, but it's all a front. Behind the mask they are someone else. Most of us can think of someone we know who we have felt has worn a Christian mask. Their behavior may not be that much worse than most people, but when coupled with their pious rhetoric and spiritual guise, the negative impact is overwhelming. Of hypocrites, Jesus said, "Everything they do is done for men to see. . . . Woe to you . . . you hypocrites! You clean the outside of the cup and dish, but inside they are full of greed and self-indulgence" (Matt. 23:5, 25).

Disappointment with the Church

It's not just Christians who disappoint, however, but their institutions as well. Few religious faiths are as intimately linked with an organization as Christianity is with the church. And more and more seekers are saying, "Spirituality, yes; Christianity, maybe; church, no."

Bored

A father asked his preschool son, who was busy with his blocks, what he was building. The little boy said, "A church, so be quiet."

The father was encouraged by that answer because he thought his son was learning to be reverent in God's house. So he said, "Why are we to be quiet in church, son?"

"Because," the boy said, "the people are all asleep."

There is a growing conviction among spiritual seekers that church is irrelevant to the way they live. Seekers come wanting to hear messages that detail what God might say to the struggle of marriage, the challenge of parenting, the dynamics of self-control, or the confusion about vocation, and they don't get it. The services themselves are often poor in quality, repetitious, lifeless, and outdated.

Burned

Not only are people bored with the church, but they've been burned by the church, personally wounded by something that happened to them or to someone they cared about. Ken Blanchard is well known for his book *The One-Minute Manager* and the many one-minute applications that have followed. Blanchard became a Christian late in his life, and in writing about that decision, he talked candidly about why he didn't pursue it earlier. As a young man, he was involved in a church near Kent State University. It was the 1960s, and there was a great deal of student unrest. In fact, Kent State was the site of one of the worst moments in that period, when the National Guard opened fire and killed four students.

The minister of the church Blanchard attended was in sympathy with the students. In fact, he joined them during their protests and their marches. That didn't go over very well with some of the more conservative members of the congregation, so they terminated his employment in a very abrupt and unkind way. Blanchard writes that anger and disillusionment came crashing in on him. He said, "If that's what church is all about, forget it." And he and his wife dropped out, and for the next fifteen years attended only at Christmas and Easter.[3]

Bickering

In the minds of many seekers, the church has also been marked by internal discord. A few years ago I read a disturbing news story on the front page of a newspaper in Louisville, Kentucky. The headline read, "Church Meeting Ends in Fray, Beleaguered Pastor Resigns Amid Turmoil." In the article, the tale of the St. Paul Missionary Baptist Church was told to the world. A situation that involved years of discord, division, and turmoil finally erupted one Sunday into fistfights between members that took over a dozen Louisville police officers to end. The reporter had every right to be sarcastic when he wrote that those "who shortly before had been lifting hands in praise of God began raising hands against one another."[4] Because of stories such as this, people look at the church and say, "Thanks, but no thanks. I've got enough problems in my life—I don't need to go to church and get more."

Beaten-Up

Fourth, people have been beaten-up. They've encountered a loveless, legalistic attitude. Michelle was a woman who was trapped in the demeaning world of prostitution, drug addiction, and alcoholism. Wanting to escape the hell on earth her life had become, Michelle disguised herself and hid from her pimp for several days while going through chemical withdrawal. She was discovered and dragged into the chambers of her raging pimp, where she was beaten until unconscious while the other prostitutes watched and learned. Next Michelle tried suicide—anything to escape the nightmare of her existence. A relative found her body, hours from death, and rushed her to the hospital where her life was saved.

This time Michelle turned to the only place she could imagine there might be hope—a local church. She had no sense of self-worth left. Used by men, rejected by the world, she turned to God's people. She knew she deserved punishment but hoped against hope she might find mercy. Halfway through the church service the pastor recognized her from her life on the street. Before the entire congregation he pointed her out and then lectured her for defiling the house of God with her filthy presence. He then ordered her out.[5] And I'm sure she left.

Business

A final concern is that the church has become too much like a business. Churches always seem to be asking for money, papering their walls with giant thermometers showing the progress of fund-raising campaigns. Seekers come and go, sensing that the church is more interested in their wallets than in them.

Dealing with the Disappointment

Disappointment with Christians is very real to those who seek, and very confusing. When those who claim to follow

Christ are immoral, inflexible, strange, uptight, unloving, judgmental, or hypocritical, it casts shadows on the faith itself. And when our experience with a Christian community involves being bored, or even worse, burned, it is tempting to walk away from Christianity altogether. Yet disappointed people who continue their exploration of the Christian faith have often done so by reminding themselves of the following spiritual truths.

Christians Are Not Perfect

First, while somewhat trite, the phrase "Christians are not perfect, just forgiven" is important to remember. What is behind many—not all, but many—charges and accusations against the character and integrity of Christians is the demand for perfection in the life of anyone who claims to be a Christian and urges others to consider Christianity. If a Christian slips up in any way, the charge is instantly, "Hypocrite! I thought you were supposed to be a Christian!"

Yet this charge is unfair on two fronts: First, it is not an accurate understanding of what it means to enter into the Christian life, and second, it is not the true meaning of a hypocrite. Authentic Christians have made the decision to believe in and follow Christ. They have chosen to turn away from their willful disobedience and rebellion against God and accept what Jesus did on the cross as the payment for their sins and the means of forgiveness from God. These people have then invited God's leadership into their life and have begun the journey of walking under God's management. But nowhere in this series of events does one reach perfection or sinlessness.

Hypocrites, on the other hand, are people who consciously and purposefully wear masks. They knowingly and intentionally talk one way and act another. They are counterfeit Christians. As a seeker, you have every right to reject their "faith," for it is not faith at all. But a hypocrite is not the same as a Christian who fails to meet your expectations, or a Christian whom you "catch" sinning one day. If you were to come and spend a day with me, I can assure you I would disappoint you. I love my wife, but you would see how I fail daily in being the husband I'm supposed to be. I love my four children, but you would witness the countless times I am insensitive and impatient. I also love God, and urge others to do the same, but if you want to see someone who fails to live consistently the life he knows he *ought* to live, I would be an excellent candidate.

But the truth runs even deeper. As a Christian, I remain a sinner who struggles with sin and often loses. All Christians do. Alexander Whyte, a Christian leader in nineteenth-century Scotland, was once approached by a woman who showered praise on him and his life. With appropriate honesty, Whyte said, "Madam, if you knew the man I really was, you would spit in my face."[6]

Does such imperfection mean that all Christians are simply counterfeits? Only if you believe that authentic Christianity demands perfection. This, however, would be a gross misunderstanding of the Christian faith. Christians are imperfect human beings trying to live a life with Christ, often failing at that task on a daily basis. Yet the longer they authentically try to journey with Christ in a spirit of obedience and submission, the more their lives reflect his life. For example, you may observe that a particular Christian woman you know—let's call her Fran—has a much more difficult time keeping away from gossip than a non-Christian woman you know, whom we will call Betty. But such observations have little to do with whether Christianity works or if it is true. The question is what would Fran be like if she were *not* in a relationship with Christ, and what would Betty be like if she *was?*[7]

At this point some might say, "Well, I don't think Christians ought to be perfect, but they ought to have this area down!" and then they cite the one area of life that they think anyone who claims to be a Christian should maintain with perfection. The problem is that everyone has a different expectation of what that area should be. For one, it may be finances, for another, marriage, and for a third, parenting. You add them up, and the expectation of perfection is back in action. When you become a Christian, you begin the process of being transformed more and more into the likeness of Christ. God gives you a clean slate in terms of your past history and then sets you on the path toward becoming more and more like him. Look at what the apostle Paul wrote to Timothy on this subject:

> Christ Jesus came into the world to save sinners—of whom I am the worst. But for that very reason I was shown mercy so that in me, the worst of sinners, Christ Jesus might display his unlimited patience as an example for those who would believe on him and receive eternal life.
>
> 1 Timothy 1:15–16

Christians are not cured of all sin and imperfection, but in becoming Christians, they have clearly entered the hospital for treatment. As a result, most Christians have had their lives changed in such a way that when you look at them, you find that their relationship with Christ has had a profound, positive influence on their lives. There are those who are farther along the path of recovery than others, and some who are better at following the prescribed treatment than others, but make no mistake, all are being treated for sin-sickness and exhibit all the symptoms.[8]

The Church Is to Be the New Community

This leads to a second thought. While the church is often dysfunctional in its expression of community, it has a clear and compelling vision that is leading it on a daily basis toward health and wholeness in a way unlike any other gathering. Jesus came to establish a new community of people. He said, "I will build *my* church" (Matt. 16:18, emphasis added).

Jesus wanted the church to be an authentic community, full of people who are allowed and encouraged to be real with each other, opening themselves up for care and love and support. The new community that Jesus initiated was to be built on healthy, deep, loving relationships that are forged on the anvil of conflict resolution. The new community Jesus came to establish was to be marked by a spirit of acceptance, one that looks at people, imperfections and all, and accepts them for who they are and how God made them. In essence, Jesus wanted the church to be a place where people could love and be loved, know and be known, serve and be served, and celebrate and be celebrated.

Most seekers find that when they explore the vision for church that Jesus and the Bible describe, it isn't church itself they are turned off to but the way people have been doing church. And while many churches fall short of this vision, countless others are decisively marked by the biblical portrait of the church as the new community. Seekers who find such churches not only discover the community that they have longed for but an atmosphere of acceptance that encourages their spiritual pilgrimage toward God.[9]

Christians Should Not Stand in the Way of Your Relationship with Christ

The third consideration for those who seek, and perhaps the most important of all, is this: Disappointing Christians and the churches in which they gather should not stand in the way of your relationship with Christ. The real issue is Jesus, not the weaknesses and imperfections or behavior of those who try to follow him.

Imagine that one of the local elementary schools in your area decides it wants its students to perform Beethoven's Fifth Symphony. You have never heard the work but have often heard of it, so you buy a ticket and plan to attend. Now when you go and hear the concert by those elementary students, would it be fair or even reasonable for you to assess the worth and brilliance of Beethoven's masterpiece based on that performance? Most people familiar with the work would warn you, saying, "Don't be too quick to make up your mind about Beethoven based on that concert. They're just kids. They'll probably butcher it." In essence, they would be saying that the elementary school performance of Beethoven's Fifth Symphony has nothing to do with the actual brilliance of Beethoven's music. And they would be right.[10]

There are a lot of Christians walking around trying to live

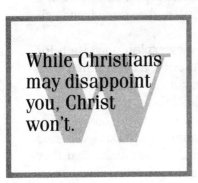

While Christians may disappoint you, Christ won't.

for Jesus, myself included, who are like elementary school kids attempting Beethoven's Fifth Symphony. Don't judge the composer *or* the music by our performance! Our failure at living the way Jesus lived should have nothing to do with your dealings with Jesus, much less the truth of his message. As the great nineteenth-century Russian novelist Leo Tolstoy, who was a Christian, wrote in a personal letter,

> Attack me, I do this myself, but attack me rather than the path I follow and which I point out to anyone who asks me where I think it lies. If I know the way home and am walking along it drunkenly, is it any less the right way because I am staggering from side to side![11]

There will be disappointment with Christians as long as there are imperfect people. Since all Christians are imperfect, there will always be disappointment. You may have been deeply wounded by people who have claimed to be Christians but who were only wearing masks. Such hypocrites can be an easy excuse for turning away from the Christian faith. But while Christians may disappoint you, Christ won't. Remember, no matter who plays it, the Fifth Symphony is still a pretty good piece of music.

BUT WILL IT WORK?

Scott Peck opened his best-selling book, *The Road Less Traveled,* with a short but profound sentence: "Life is difficult." And he was right—life *is* difficult. This leads many seekers to begin their spiritual search not for the discovery of truth but for the discovery of coping strategies and survival skills for making it through another day. As one man said to me, "I care about whether or not it's all true, but to be honest, right now in my life I care more about whether or not it will *work*." Does Christianity work? Is it a faith that, when applied to your life, actually helps? Christians would answer with a resounding yes but would quickly add that Christianity isn't true because it works; it works because it's true.

A Compelling Model

Christianity begins its practical relevance for the human life with Jesus, who provides a working, compelling model of how life is meant to be lived. By demonstrating what we ought to be like, Jesus showed us who we were meant to be. Jesus said,

113

> Are you tired? Worn out? Burned out on religion? Come to
> me. Get away with me and you'll recover your life. I'll show
> you how to take a real rest. Walk with me and work with me—
> watch how I do it. Learn the unforced rhythms of grace. I
> won't lay anything heavy or ill-fitting on you. Keep company
> with me and you'll learn to live freely and lightly.
>
> Matthew 11:28–30 TM

The practical value of such a model cannot be underesti-
mated. Optimal growth occurs when you develop a relationship with someone who knows something you don't or
has experience in an area you don't and is willing to share
what they know with you. For example, a married couple will
tell you of the benefit of a counselor. An athlete will talk about
the importance of a trainer or a coach. When it comes to
spiritual things, few can match the mentoring and modeling
provided by Jesus.

A Relevant Handbook

Second, Christianity has the most relevant, comprehen-
sive handbook for life that has ever been written: the Bible.
Its pages are bursting with relevance for every aspect of life,
including marriage, parenting, relationships, finances, business, self-image, and family life. The practical dynamic of
the Bible was captured in the writings of the apostle Paul,
who noted that:

> The whole Bible was given to us by inspiration from God and
> is useful to teach us what is true and to make us realize what
> is wrong in our lives; it straightens us out and helps us do
> what is right. It is God's way of making us well prepared at
> every point.
>
> 2 Timothy 3:16–17 TLB

People who have read the Bible and faithfully applied its wisdom to their lives say that its influence has been nothing less

than transformational. They will tell you it has helped them save their marriage. It has helped them straighten out their finances. It has helped them repair their broken relationships.

In the Bible we read, "Despise God's Word and find yourself in trouble. Obey it and succeed" (Prov. 13:13 TLB). This should not be overlooked by a spiritual seeker. In examining the Christian faith, the Bible's practical advice and insight on life should be tested. Try applying the Bible's principles to your life, and see for yourself the impact they can have on daily living.

A Present Power

One summer my family and I vacationed at Emerald Isle, North Carolina. Near Emerald Isle is a little town called Beaufort. It is one of the oldest towns in North Carolina and is rich in history. You can take a tour of several buildings that date back as far as 1706. One of the buildings is an apothecary. During the tour, we saw all kinds of wonder drugs, guaranteed to cure anything you had, that were sold between one hundred and two hundred years ago. There was "Oil of Youth," and on the side of the bottle was a list of its ingredients: 2 percent ether, 4 percent chloroform, and 60 percent alcohol. It said you could take it internally or apply it externally, and it promised to cure asthma, fever, coughing, colds, diarrhea, kidney trouble, and nerves. At 60 percent alcohol, I'll bet it *did* help one's nerves! We saw "Dr. DeWitt's Eclectic Remedy" for cramps and a bottle labeled "Blood Syrup," which was a tonic that was supposed to heal the liver, clean the blood, tone the stomach, open pores, and regulate bowels. Sales of the remedies were high because people then— as now—intuitively knew that they needed something outside of themselves to address the complexities of their lives.

Christianity offers this outside element, but it is not in the form of an elixir. It is the very power of God. In Ephesians, Paul says, "I pray that you will begin to understand how incredibly great [God's] power is to help those who believe him. It is that same mighty power that raised Christ from the dead" (Eph. 1:19–20 TLB). The incredible power of God—strong enough to raise Christ from the dead—is available to help those who have turned their lives over to Christ. And we need power—not only to endure the stress and struggle of life but to experience lasting, authentic life change in the areas of our weaknesses.

> The incredible power of God—strong enough to raise Christ from the dead—is available to help those who have turned their lives over to Christ.

We all have problems—problems with our marriages, problems with our finances, problems at work, problems with our kids. Christianity says that the power to change our lives can come from God. We don't have it within us to live the way we want to live, much less the way we are supposed to live. But the Bible says that the very same power that raised Jesus from the dead is available for our lives. That's why the apostle Paul was able to say, "I have the strength to face all conditions by the power that Christ gives me" (Phil. 4:13 GNB). Most of us have learned that we can't live life on our own—that we need help. Christianity contends that God is alive and well and active and that beginning a relationship with him is like finally plugging our cord into the electrical socket and receiving what we've always missed out on before: the power for life change.

An Astounding Track Record

Finally, Christianity has an astounding track record. Just consider the impact it has made in the lives of millions of

Christians throughout time and history. There are countless people with amazing stories that provide a towering confirmation of the power the Christian faith holds for life in the real world.

A woman lived in a state-run convalescent center that was large, understaffed, and overflowing with senile, helpless, lonely people waiting to die. On the brightest of days the center seemed dark and smelled of sickness and urine.

One Mother's Day, a man named Tom Schmidt went there, wanting to reach out and serve at least one person. He had a flower that he wanted to give to an overlooked mother. Soon he found himself in a hallway where he seemed to find the worst cases—people tied onto carts or into wheelchairs and looking completely helpless. And at the end of the hallway, he saw an old woman strapped in a wheelchair.

It was obvious she was blind. The large hearing aid over one ear told him that she was almost deaf. One side of her face was being eaten by cancer. There was a discolored and running sore covering part of her cheek, and it had pushed her nose to one side, dropped one eye, and distorted her jaw so that what should have been the corner of her mouth was the bottom of her mouth. Because of the deformity, she drooled constantly.

Tom was later told that when new nurses arrived, the supervisors would send them in to feed this woman, thinking that if they could stand the sight of her, they could survive anything in the building. He also learned that this woman was eighty-nine years old and that she had been there, bedridden, blind, nearly deaf, and alone, for twenty-five years.

Her name was Mabel.

Tom didn't know why he spoke to her; she didn't look as though she could even respond to him. But he put the flower in her hand and said, "Here is a flower for you. Happy Mother's Day."

She held the flower up to her face and tried to smell it, and then she spoke. Much to his surprise, her words, although somewhat garbled because of her deformity, were obviously produced by a clear mind. She said, "Thank you. It's lovely. But may I give it to someone else? I can't see it, you know. I'm blind."

He said, "Of course," and then pushed her in her wheelchair back down the hallway to a place where he thought they could find some alert patients. They found one, and he stopped the chair.

Mabel held out the flower and said, "Here, this is from Jesus." That was when it dawned on Tom that this was not an ordinary human being, and as he began to talk to her, he found out why.

Mabel had grown up on a small farm that she had managed with her mother until her mother died. Then she had run the farm by herself until 1950, when her blindness and sickness sent her to the convalescent ward. For twenty-five years she had gotten progressively weaker and sicker, with constant headaches, backaches, and stomachaches, and then the cancer came. Her three roommates were all human vegetables who would scream occasionally but never talk. They often soiled their bedclothes, and because the hospital was understaffed, the stench was often overpowering in the room where Mabel lived.

Tom and Mabel became friends, and he visited her once or twice a week for the next three years. Some days he read to her from the Bible, and often when he paused, she would continue reciting the passage from memory, word for word. On other days, he took a book of hymns and sang with her, and she knew all the words to the old songs. For Mabel, these were not merely exercises in memory. She often stopped mid-hymn and made a brief comment about lyrics she considered particularly relevant to her own situation. Tom said he never heard her speak of loneliness or pain except in the stress she placed on certain lines as she sang the hymns.

It wasn't long before Tom turned from a sense of being helpful to a sense of wonder, and he carried a pen and paper so he could write down the things she said. During one particularly hectic week, when his mind seemed to be torn in ten different directions with all the things he had to think about, he wondered what Mabel had to think about—hour after hour, day after day, week after week, not even knowing whether it was day or night. So he asked her, "Mabel, what do you think about when you lie here?"

And she said, "I think about my Jesus."

He sat there and thought for a moment about how difficult it was for him to think about Jesus for even five minutes, and then he asked, "*What* do you think about Jesus?"

She replied slowly and carefully, and Tom wrote down what she said. "I think about how good he's been to me. He's been awfully good to me in my life, you know. I'm one of those kind who's mostly satisfied. Lots of folks wouldn't care much for what I think. Lots of folks would think I'm kind of old-fashioned. But I don't care. I'd rather have Jesus. He's all the world to me."

And then Mabel began to sing a hymn:
"Jesus is all the world to me,
My life, my joy, my all.
He is my strength from day to day,
Without him I would fall.
When I am sad, to him I go,
No other one can cheer me so.
When I am sad he makes me glad.
He's my friend."[1]

This story is not fiction. Incredible as it may seem, a human being lived like this. How could she do it? In the face of more pain and tragedy and suffering than you and I will most likely ever face, how could she do it? She's already told us: Jesus intersected the deepest needs of her life and transformed her from the inside out. Here was an ordinary human being who received supernatural power to live in an extraordinary way.

And the promise of the Christian life is that such a life is possible for all human beings—a life in the presence and under the power of the living God.

What Will You Rely On?

Determining where to place your trust and what you are going to rely on when it comes to life's challenges is decisive. In the first of the Ten Commandments, the Bible records the following declaration: "I am the LORD your God. . . . You shall have no other gods before me" (Exod. 20:2–3). This commandment is not a concession that other gods exist whom humans can encounter and engage in relationship. What this commandment is teaching is that we can choose to put our trust in something or someone other than God. But God says, "Put *me* first. Build your life on *me*. Nothing else you might choose to build your life on will help you when you need it most."

At some point, we all have trouble. Life is difficult. We all have needs, experience crises, and encounter tragedies. We all have times when life falls apart. If we look to something or someone for help that cannot come through for us, help will not come. We can place our trust in things other than God: careers, mutual funds, the way we look, a particular position or title or degree, physical pleasure, marriage or family. These become the "gods" we look to for help and security and happiness. Yet the Bible teaches that these things will not come through for us when we need them most:

> Our God is in heaven. . . .
> Their idols are silver and gold,
>   made by the hands of men.
> They have mouths, but cannot speak,
>   eyes, but they cannot see;
> they have ears, but cannot hear,
>   noses, but they cannot smell;

they have hands, but cannot feel,
feet, but they cannot walk;
nor can they utter a sound with their throats.
Those who make them will be like them,
and so will all who trust in them.

Psalm 115:3–8

The question "Does it work?" is crucial, because whatever we are counting on to work for us needs to deliver in our times of need. If we have built our lives on something that will not come through for us when we need it most, then we have built our lives on something that does not work. Christianity does not ask us to build our lives on a faith that is divorced from the needs of the real world. Instead, it provides a compelling model, a relevant handbook, a power that is present and available, and an astounding track record of proven performance. Bottom line: It works. Why? Because it's true.

13

Stop Signs for Seekers

There was a moment—just a moment—before I got married when I thought to myself, *What in the world am I doing?* In that moment I thought of all the things I'd be giving up or changing—forever. Like dating. Never again would I be able to see an attractive, appealing woman and have the freedom to pursue the relationship. Once married, I would probably have to fold my underwear, screw the top back on the toothpaste, put my dirty clothes in a basket, and spend my day off going to fabric stores. I wouldn't be able to go out with my friends, stay out all night, or take off on a skiing trip. What if I couldn't keep it up? Marriage was for life, at least I knew that was the way it was supposed to be.

So for a moment—just a moment—I panicked and became very unsure that getting married was a smart thing to do. Now, I cannot imagine life apart from my wife. What I have experienced over the many years of marriage far outweighs anything I may have sacrificed by entering into that commitment. I am not less of a person but more of a person. I do not think in terms of lost freedom or opportunity but in terms of what I have gained through my relationship with my wife. My marriage has been very real with its share of struggles and conflicts, but it has also been very, very good.

Making a spiritual commitment is like any other commitment—it is often accompanied by a host of fears and anxieties related to the decision. If you don't have *any* fears, you may need to dig deeper into the dynamics of the commitment. Perhaps you aren't understanding the commitment fully or taking it seriously enough. Once, when Jesus was being followed by a large crowd of people who were eager to commit, he turned around, stopped them, and challenged them:

> If you want to be my follower you must love me more than your own father and mother, wife and children, brothers and sisters—yes, more than your own life. Otherwise, you cannot be my disciple. And you cannot be my disciple if you do not carry your own cross and follow me.
>
> But don't begin until you count the cost.
>
> Luke 14:26–28 NLT

Jesus was clear: Do not make a spiritual decision or commitment blindly, naively, or superficially. Make a decision, but don't ever do it unthinkingly or impulsively or in a way that doesn't count the cost. Spiritual commitment is serious business.

On the other hand, it is also a mistake to come to a point of decision and then let fears and anxieties rule the day. Those who seek should honestly evaluate each concern to determine if it means

> **Those who seek should honestly evaluate each concern to determine if it means they should turn away from the commitment, or if they should turn away from the fear instead.**

they should turn away from the commitment, or if they should turn away from the fear instead. With that in mind, let's look at some of the stop signs for seekers.

Unanswered Questions

It is very common to go into a spiritual holding pattern because you still have questions that haven't been answered. You want to be sure, beyond any doubt, of what is true and best. The dilemma, however, is that your spiritual search is for God, and the depth of God can never be fully explored, much less understood. You will *always* have unanswered questions because your subject is God! Therefore, the goal of any spiritual search is not to find *every* answer but *enough* answers. The line of faith can be reasonably and responsibly crossed when you come to that point in your spiritual pilgrimage when you realize that it will take more faith *not* to believe in the claims of Christ than *to* believe in the claims of Christ.

A Loss of Control

Some seekers do not make the commitment to Christ because they're afraid of what they'll have to give up. You may think that if God were allowed to lead, you would have to give up control of your life, and self-control is often our ultimate goal in life. When we're teenagers, we dream of getting out from underneath the control of our parents. In college, we can't wait to get away from the control of the rules of the university and the academic guidelines of our professors. When we enter the workforce, we dream of financial independence so that we won't be under the control of our supervisors. Our whole life is spent trying to get away from the control of others!

There can be little doubt that a relationship with Christ includes the leadership of Christ. The Christian life involves giving up control. But rather than a loss of freedom, it means a gain of competent direction. When I board a plane, I gladly give control to the pilots. I don't want to be in control, because I know that it is much better for them to guide and direct the plane. They are infinitely better qualified, and therefore, it is best to give control over to them. By doing this, do I lose anything? No, I simply gain the benefit of their competence for my life. This is what Christians believe concerning the dynamics of God's leadership, accepting what the Bible says: "Trust in the LORD with all your heart and lean not on your own understanding; in all your ways acknowledge him, and he will make your paths straight" (Prov. 3:5–6).

True freedom is not in conflict with being led. Just as a fish is not truly free outside the water, we do not experience true freedom apart from God's direction for our lives. I could demand the freedom to fly the plane, but such "freedom" would only cause the flight to end in disaster.

No More Fun

Perhaps you have delayed making a commitment to Christ because you think you will have to give up having a good time. As mentioned in an earlier chapter, God is sometimes seen as the cosmic cop. Perhaps you're afraid God will always be on the lookout, and if he sees you having fun, he'll say, "Hey, you! Yeah, you! Cut it out!" When you walk out of a video store, you're afraid you might hear a voice from heaven saying, "All right, what's it rated . . . PG-13? Hand it over, nice and slow."

I felt this way for many years, believing that Christians who were serious about their faith would also have to be extremely boring. I discovered that Jesus isn't like that at all. In fact, one of the Bible's writers described his lifestyle in these terms: "The Son of Man [Jesus] came, enjoying life" (Matt. 11:19 PHILLIPS). His promise to those who choose to follow him is just as encouraging. He said, "I have come that they may have life, and have it to the full" (John 10:10). The life of Jesus demonstrates that what God wants to do is show us how to have fun that isn't destructive to our lives. He wants to free us from the negative side effects of the unrestrained pursuit of pleasure that will end in pain. This means gaining a sensitivity to those activities and pursuits that are harmful to us.

Most of us have heard of the disease called leprosy. According to Dr. Paul Brand, a specialist in the field, what makes leprosy so terrible is that it eliminates a person's ability to feel pain. Because leprosy destroys the nerves that alert one to pain, the disease makes its victims devastatingly susceptible and vulnerable to injury. Brand writes that individuals with leprosy would come to him for treatment with missing fingers, ulcerated feet, clawed hands—all as a result of the loss of sensation.[1] God is the God of pleasure and fun, and he is delighted for us to enjoy life. But he wants us to learn how to have fun without harming ourselves or others. The leadership that God wants to give our lives doesn't destroy the "good" life but enables it by helping us grow in our knowledge of the things that cause pain.

What Will My Friends Think?

A very large issue for many seekers has to do with relationships—simply put, what will friends and family think? A decision to pursue a faith with commitment—particularly one that may be different from the faith of those who matter most to us—can hold enormous consequences. If your family is Jewish, Islamic, Jehovah's Witness, or Mormon, choosing Christianity may be seen as an act of familial treason. If your spouse is openly antagonistic toward spiritual things, it may seem as though a commitment to Christ means inviting more stress into your marriage.

When I chose to commit my life to Christ's leadership, none of my friends understood it at all. I was in college, and I remember going home to my roommate, Mike, and waking him up. That wasn't a particularly smart thing to do. Mike threw the hammer, discus, and shotput for the college track team, and when I woke him up, he had every right to throw me! Though Mike later turned over leadership of his life to Christ, that night as I shared my decision with him, he just stared at me as though I were from another planet. After processing it for a minute, he said, "Does this mean we have to throw the beer out?" Leave it to Mike to cut to the chase on the important issues of life.

After that, my life went through—and needed to go through—a 180-degree turnaround. There were times when my new faith produced awkward moments of adjustment for those closest to me, but it didn't end a single relationship. If anything, it strengthened my relationships. This is not, however, always the case. When people go on a spiritual search and find what they were looking for, it changes their lives and the lives of those around them. This life change can be extremely threatening to those who do not feel led to make similar changes or commitments. Our tendency is to ridicule or reject that which threatens us, which can be very painful to the person who is ridiculed or rejected. You must ask whether the momentary difficulties and tensions are worth it. Jesus thought so, even promising that "everyone who has left houses or brothers or sisters or father or mother or children or fields for my sake will receive a hundred times as much and will inherit eternal life" (Matt. 19:29).

What If I Can't Keep It Up?

Nobody wants to start something or do something that draws attention and then not be able to stay committed and follow through with it. In our minds, it would have been better not to have done anything at all. So we don't.

One of the biggest stop signs is looking at the Christian life and saying, "I don't think I could keep it up." But feeling that way is a huge misunderstanding of what Christianity is all about and misses two very important truths about the Christian faith.

The First Missed Truth

The first truth that is missed is this: Becoming a Christian is not about committing and following through. Commitment is a noble effort, and Christians are called to be deeply, deeply committed, but that's not what becoming a Christian is all about, nor is it at the heart of what *being* a Christian is all about. When it comes to spiritual things, God knows you can't keep your commitment. God knows you can't follow through. If that's what it took to become a Christian and stay a Christian, nobody would ever be a Christian. At least not for very long.

You say, "Well, what about how I'm living? I don't want to be a hypocrite!"

No, and God doesn't want you to be a hypocrite either. But remember what a hypocrite is. A hypocrite is someone who tries to project an image of living a certain way but doesn't do so. It has nothing to do with someone who comes to Christ and authentically begins trying to live according to his leadership. Of course you'll fail—all Christians do—but the Bible says to come just as you are, receive God's gift of a personal relationship, and then let him begin the transformation process. God knows you'll make mistakes. He just wants you to let him start where you are.

The Second Missed Truth

This leads to the second missed truth: You are not instantly transformed. Comedian Yakov Smirnoff says that when he first came to the United States from Russia, he wasn't prepared for the incredible variety of instant products available in American grocery stores. He says, "On my first shopping trip, I saw powdered milk—you just add water, and you get milk. Then I saw powdered orange juice—you just add water, and you get orange juice. And then I saw baby powder, and I thought to myself, *What a country!*"

One of the most basic assumptions about the Christian faith, but one that the Bible says nothing about, is that life change happens instantly upon becoming a Christian. Some believe that when a person gives his or her life to Christ, there is an immediate, substantive, in-depth miraculous change in habits, attitudes, and character. The truth is that when you give your life to Christ, your eternal destiny is altered, there is a radical reorientation of priorities, there is a new life purpose, and there is the power and work of the Holy Spirit in your life. But rather than instant liberation from every bad habit or character flaw you've ever possessed, what takes place is more like the landing of an army on a beach and the routing out of the enemy as the army makes its way inland. The event of becoming a Christian is best seen as the beginning of a long journey. Just as there is a process that leads up to the event of making a decision for Christ, there is a process toward life change that begins after you make the decision.

Ignacy Paderewski, the famous composer and pianist, was scheduled to perform at a great concert hall in the United States. One of the people who came to the concert was a mother with her fidgety nine-year-old son. She had hoped that if her son heard Paderewski, he would be motivated to practice the piano. She turned away for a moment to talk with some friends, and when she did, the little guy slipped away and got up on stage. He sat down at the concert grand that had been set up for Paderewski. But that's not all! He began to play chopsticks. When he did that, the auditorium became deadly silent. The people were stunned! No one could believe what he was doing. But he just kept on playing as if he didn't even notice them. Then they began to yell, "Get that kid away from there!" "What's he doing?" "Where's his mother?" "Somebody stop him!"

The little boy suddenly realized he was the focus of attention, and his face turned beet red. He started to get up, thinking, *I've screwed up again. I can't do anything right.* Backstage, however, Paderewski overheard the shouts and quickly figured out what was happening. He grabbed his coat and ran out on stage. Without one word of announcement, he stooped over behind the boy, reached around both sides, and began to improvise a countermelody to harmonize and enhance the boy's rendition of chopsticks.

As the two of them played together, Paderewski kept whispering in the boy's ear, "Keep going. Don't quit, son. Keep on playing. Don't stop. Don't quit." And the boy didn't. When they finished, the audience burst into applause.

We all stumble on the path that God calls us to follow. We approach the piano, begin to play, and at the first taunt, want to flee the stage. It is then that God wants to come up, lean over, wrap his arms around us, and say, "Now, keep going. Don't quit. Keep on. Don't stop." And if you'll let him do that, you'll find yourself never wanting to stop playing the beautiful music God has in store for your relationship together.[2]

It Can Wait

The final stop sign may very well be the most subtle: There's just no hurry. We can deal with spiritual conclusions and commitments later. We can say to ourselves, *Listen, I'm in good health. I wear my seat belt. My car has air bags. It's not like I'm going to die tonight. I plan on dealing with it— I really do! I'm just taking my time. It's a big decision, and while I've pretty much decided on Christianity, I'm just going to sit on this for a while.*

Jesus encountered this mind-set in his day too. In fact, he told a story about it:

The ground of a certain rich man produced a good crop. He thought to himself, "What shall I do? I have no place to store my crops."

Then he said, "This is what I'll do. I will tear down my barns and build bigger ones, and there I will store all my grain and my goods. And I'll say to myself, 'You have plenty of good things laid up for many years. Take life easy; eat, drink and be merry.'"

But God said to him, "You fool! This very night your life will be demanded from you."

Luke 12:16–20

Why did Jesus tell that story? Was it because he was into scare tactics? Was he into high pressure and manipulation? No. It was because he knew that the stakes are high. It was because he knew that the death rate among human beings is still right around 100 percent and that all of us will die sooner than we expect. And once we do, it's over. Our decision has been sealed. There are no second chances.

I'll never forget hearing a story about a strategy session among some demons. They were trying to figure out how to stop people who were close to making a decision for Christ. One demon stood and shouted, "I know! We can tell them that there is no life after death!"

Satan replied, "No, that will never work. Man is not ignorant; even atheists admit that there is an eternal soul and feel that this life does not end it all."

Another demon stood and said, "I've got it! Let's say there is no God, or if there is, he's not a personal God but just a force or an energy field!"

Satan said, "That won't work either because most humans seem to intuitively know that there is a personal God—or at least want there to be."

Another said, "Let's show them all the hypocrites and all the things that have been done that have made a mockery of the name of Christ!"

"That might work for some of them," Satan replied, "but most will figure out that those people and things really have little to do with Christ himself."

Finally, a demon stood up and with a grin said, "You've all missed the most effective strategy we have."

All the demons shouted, "Tell us! Tell us!"

He said, "Tell them there is no hurry."[3]

WHEN THE SEARCH IS OVER

How will your search end? You could reject Christianity, writing off Jesus as insane or a liar and then pursue some other faith. You could abandon your spiritual search altogether as a hopeless cause that can never lead to truth. Or you could become a Christian.

Let's say you have found in Christ what you are looking for. It's been an honest, sincere search—neither impulsive nor superficial—and you're ready to go forward, to follow through on what you have found. You are ready to enter into a relationship with God through Christ. What do you do next? The Bible points to four simple but very important steps.

Step One: Own Up to the Truth about Yourself

The first step is to take a long, hard look in the mirror and own up to what God sees: someone who is precious to him but in rebellion. Admit that you have rejected his leadership and are, quite frankly, a sinner in need of a savior. No rationalizations, no cop-outs, no excuses or qualifications. The first step toward becoming a Christian involves total honesty and the self-awareness that you are a sinner before a holy God.

133

The Bible says, "If we say that we have no sin, we are only fooling ourselves, and refusing to accept the truth" (1 John 1:8 TLB). Step one: Stop fooling yourself and accept the truth.

Step Two: Be Willing to Change

Second, you must be willing to repent. The word *repent* isn't one of those words we enjoy hearing. It's a word that has often been ridiculed, even scorned. But it is a good word because of what it represents: life change.

> The first step toward becoming a Christian involves total honesty and the self-awareness that you are a sinner before a holy God.

When you repent of your sins, you are going beyond just admitting them—you are wanting to turn from them. You realize you have rebelled against a holy God, and you are sorry. You want to alter the course of your life and move away from your patterns of sinful behavior. This is why, in the Book of Acts, it says, "Repent, then, and turn to God" (Acts 3:19).

Step Three: Believe the Message

The third step involves believing the message God has given in the Bible. The message of the Bible is that Jesus was God in human form. As a man, Jesus lived a perfect life. He was kind, tender, gentle, patient, and sympathetic. He loved people. He worked miracles and taught people how to live lives that honored God. Then he died and was raised from the dead to take away the sin of the world and to become the savior of all people. The entire Bible is built around the story of Christ and his promise of eternal life to people like you and me. It was written for one purpose and one purpose only: that we would believe.[1] In fact, the Bible says that "if you confess with your mouth that Jesus is Lord and believe in your heart that God raised him from the dead, you will be saved" (Rom. 10:9 NLT).

Step Four: Receive the Gift

After you have admitted your sin, repented of it, and accepted the truth of the message of the Bible, you are ready for step four: Reach out and receive the gift of what Christ did for you through his death on the cross. And what Jesus did on the cross really is a gift. The Bible says, "For the wages of sin is death, but the gift of God is eternal life in Christ Jesus our Lord" (Rom. 6:23). You should have been on the cross. I should have been on the cross. But God, in his love and mercy, chose to provide a way out. He forgave our sins through the full payment of our sin penalty, and this opened the door for us to be restored to a relationship with God. That's why Paul wrote, "Saving is all his idea, and all his work. All we do is trust him enough to let him do it. It's God's gift from start to finish!" (Eph. 2:8–9 TM). But because it is a gift, it must be received. It can be offered, but it isn't yours until you reach out and take it.

At the end of your search, when you come face to face with Christ, there is one and only one question that must be answered: Will you admit, repent, believe, and then receive the gift of salvation and a relationship with God through Christ? Saying yes is just one prayer away because the Bible says that "everyone who calls on the name of the Lord will be saved" (Rom. 10:13).

If you want to take that final step and become a Christian, here is how you can pray: First, begin by admitting to God that you are a sinner. Tell him you know you fall short of his standards, his holiness, his character. Then tell him you want to be forgiven for those sins, that you want a clean slate, a new beginning, a past that has been erased. Next, tell him you want his leadership in your life. You want to find out how he wants you to live, and then you want to live that way—under his direction. Finally, thank him for doing it! Thank him for forgiving you, for the leadership he is going to provide in your life, and for the relationship he is beginning with you.

If you pray that prayer and really mean it, you have become a Christian. Bells and sirens may not go off, but something miraculous and of eternal significance has taken place. Your life will never be the same.

If you give your life to Christ, I encourage you to do two things: First, tell someone! Maybe it is the person who steered you toward this book, or a Christian friend or family member—but let someone know who will celebrate this decision with you. Second, find a good church that will welcome you and help you grow in your knowledge of and love for God and your involvement with his mission.

A Final Word

For those of you who are not ready to commit to Christianity, please keep seeking. Don't stop the search! It is the most important search of your life, and one that you hopefully will not end until you have found a relationship with God. I believe that Jesus was God in human form who came to show us the way to that relationship. My hope and prayer is that this book helps you toward that same conclusion.

NOTES

Chapter 1

1. These stories are based on actual testimonies that Mark and Kristi gave at Mecklenburg Community Church, the church that aided them in their spiritual journeys. They gave permission for their names to be used and their stories to be told.

2. Wade Clark Roof, *A Generation of Seekers* (New York: Harper and Row, 1993).

3. Douglas Coupland, *Life after God* (New York: Pocket Books, 1994), 359.

Chapter 2

1. Philip Yancey, *The Jesus I Never Knew* (Grand Rapids: Zondervan, 1995), 17.

2. Adapted from Wilbur Rees, "$3.00 Worth of God," quoted in Tim Hansel, *When I Relax I Feel Guilty* (Elgin, Ill.: David C. Cook, 1979), 49.

3. An excellent Bible is *The Journey* (Grand Rapids: Zondervan/Willow Creek Resources, 1996), which is the entire text of the Bible in the New International Version. *The Journey* has been uniquely designed, with notes and insights woven into the text, to help spiritual seekers explore Christianity and better understand God.

Chapter 3

1. For the full story of Lee's journey, see his book *Inside the Mind of Unchurched Harry and Mary* (Grand Rapids: Zondervan, 1995).

2. George Barna, *What Americans Believe* (Ventura, Calif.: Regal, 1991), 200–201.

3. James Patterson and Peter Kim, *The Day America Told the Truth* (New York: Prentice Hall, 1991), 203.

4. For a thorough treatment of the debate between theists and atheists, see J. P. Moreland and Kai Nielsen, eds., *Does God Exist?* (Amherst, N.Y.: Prometheus Books, 1993).

5. Carl Sagan, *Cosmos* (New York: Random House, 1980), 4.

6. On this, see Robert Jastrow, *God and the Astronomers,* 2d ed. (New York: W. W. Norton, 1992), as well as Hugh Ross, *The Creator and the Cosmos* (Colorado Springs: NavPress, 1993).

7. Even if the universe is eternal into the future, as some physicists theorize, it is becoming widely accepted that the universe cannot avoid having a beginning. On this, see Arvind Borde and Alexander Vilenkin, "Eternal Inflation and the Initial Singularity," *Physical Review Letters* 72 (1994): 3305–9.

8. As noted in Fred Heeren, *Show Me God: What the Message from Space Is Telling Us about God* (Wheeling, Ill.: Searchlight Publications, 1995), 139. Smoot's quote was cited in Milton Rothman, "What Went Before?" *Free Inquiry* 13, no. 1 (winter 1992–1993): 12.

9. Jastrow, *God and the Astronomers,* 14.

10. Uncomfortable with the implications of this, Hawking wrote his surprisingly successful *A Brief History of Time: From the Big Bang to Black Holes* (New York: Bantam, 1988), in which he suggested the idea that time can be bounded in the past and yet not come into existence abruptly as a singularity. This is a new twist on the idea that the universe is eternal. While imaginative, it is nothing more than an untestable metaphysical theory and as beyond experimental verification as the positing of a Creator God. Many have determined that Hawking, along with many other physicists,

is simply wanting to posit a nonsupernatural "escape hatch" to avoid dealing with the implications of what science has determined. On this, see Phillip E. Johnson, *Reason in the Balance: The Case against Naturalism in Science, Law and Education* (Downers Grove, Ill.: InterVarsity Press, 1995).

11. Alan H. Guth, *The Inflationary Universe* (Reading, Mass.: Addison-Wesley, 1997), 276. Guth believes that because the energy stored in the gravitational field is represented by a negative number, it is conceivable that the total energy of the universe is zero, thus allowing for the universe to have come into existence from absolutely nothing in a manner consistent with all known conservation laws. He admits, however, that this is pure speculation beyond the realm of experimental substantiation. Even further, he concedes that it would not be from absolute nothingness—there would be a vacuum of some sorts, plus the existence of the laws of physics, thus forcing the question once again: From whence did these laws come?

12. Jastrow, *God and the Astronomers*, 107. This begs the question of who, then, made God? We ask this because we live in space and time, and nothing in our understanding of space and time can exist independent of some type of beginning. So if God began our universe, who began God? The Christian response is to challenge the presupposition of the question, namely, that God is confined to our understandings of space and time. The Bible points to God as the creator of space and time, independent of its constraints. God is eternal, without beginning or end, and is not limited to our understandings of beginning or ending.

13. Plato believed that "the order of the motion of stars" would "lead men to believe in the gods" (*Laws* 12.966e).

14. William Paley, *Natural Theology*, 12th ed. (Lincoln-Rembrandt Publishing), 1–3.

15. Sir Fred Hoyle, *The Intelligent Universe* (London: Michael Joseph, 1983), 11–12, 19, 251. I am indebted to Hoyle for the inspiration for my space shuttle illustration, which he discussed in terms of an airplane.

16. Fred Hoyle and Chandra Wickramasinghe, *Evolution from Space* (London: J. M. Dent and Sons, 1981), 24.

17. Stephen Hawking, quoted in John Boslough, *Masters of Time: Cosmology at the End of Innocence* (New York: Addison-Wesley, 1992), 55.

18. Hawking, *A Brief History of Time,* 127.

19. As cited in Luis Palau, *God Is Relevant* (New York: Doubleday, 1997), 32.

20. Paul Davies, *The Mind of God* (New York: Simon and Schuster, 1992), 232. Even if life on another planet, such as Mars, is verified, the miraculous origin of life is not diminished, for nowhere does the Bible intimate that God created life on this planet alone.

21. Michael J. Behe, *Darwin's Black Box: The Biochemical Challenge to Evolution* (New York: The Free Press, 1996), 4. This is different from the ability some types of living organisms have for variation when moved to different environments, a process called microevolution, which has been fairly well documented.

22. On this, see Richard Dawkins, *The Blind Watchmaker* (New York: W. W. Norton, 1996).

23. Charles Darwin, *Origin of Species,* 6th ed. (New York: New York University Press, 1988), 154.

24. Behe, *Darwin's Black Box,* 42–48.

25. Further, mutation cannot account for such development either, for while mutation can cause variation on a theme, it cannot produce an altogether different "thing." For example, Behe gives the following analogy in *Darwin's Black Box:* "A mutation is a change in *one* of the lines of instructions. So instead of saying, 'Take a 1/4-inch nut,' a mutation might say, 'Take a 3/8-inch nut.' . . . What a mutation *cannot* do is change all the instructions in one step—say, to build a fax machine instead of a radio" (41). Intriguingly, Darwin himself noted that "to suppose that the eye with all its inimitable contrivances for adjusting the focus to different distances, for admitting different amounts of light, and for the correction of spherical and chromatic aberration, could have been formed by natural selection, seems, I freely confess, absurd in the

highest degree" (Charles Darwin, "Difficulties with the Theory," *Origins of Species,* Great Books of the Western World, ed. Robert Maynard Hutchins, vol. 49 [Chicago: Encyclopaedia Britannica, Inc., 1952], 85).

26. Behe, *Darwin's Black Box,* 232.

27. It should be noted that challenging Darwinian evolution in no way forces one into a "young-earth" position. On this, see Hugh Ross, *Creation and Time* (Colorado Springs: NavPress, 1994). Further, it does not deny the fossil record of primitive ape-like creatures, just the interpretation given to their existence as evidence of hominoid evolution. (We have ape-like creatures even today. They're called apes.) Recent DNA tests further support this conclusion, finding that Neanderthals were not close relatives or even ancestral forms of existing people. On this, see *Washington Post* reporter Curt Suplee, "Scientists Using DNA Say Neanderthals Are Not Ancestors of Modern Mankind," *Charlotte Observer,* 11 July 1997, p. 6A. For a full and stimulating challenge to the idea of Darwinian evolution, see Phillip E. Johnson, *Darwin on Trial* (Downers Grove, Ill.: InterVarsity Press, 1991).

28. Augustine, *Confessions,* I.i.1, trans. Henry Chadwick (Oxford: Oxford University Press, 1991), 3.

29. The idea dates at least as far back as Ludwig Feuerbach in the 1830s but was popularized by Sigmund Freud in *The Future of an Illusion* in *Complete Psychological Works,* vol. 2 (London: Hogarth, 1953). Many have noted that Freud's ideas come more from his own atheistic prejudices than from hard experimental evidence of his own discipline.

30. On this, see C. S. Lewis, *Mere Christianity* (New York: Macmillan, 1952), 3–7. For a detailed discussion, see Basil Mitchell, *Morality: Secular and Religious* (Oxford: Clarendon, 1980), as well as Immanuel Kant's *Critique of Practical Reason.*

31. Lewis, *Mere Christianity,* 31.

32. For further study on the implications between the choice for theism versus atheism, see Ravi Zacharias, *A Shattered Visage: The Real Face of Atheism* (Grand Rapids: Baker, 1990).

Chapter 4

1. As cited in Philip Yancey, *The Jesus I Never Knew* (Grand Rapids: Zondervan, 1995), 264. For helpful introductions to the biblical view of God, see Bill Hybels, *The God You're Looking For* (Nashville: Thomas Nelson, 1997), and J. I. Packer, *Knowing God* (Downers Grove, Ill.: InterVarsity Press, 1973).

2. Some believe the Bible presents two portraits of God: the God of the Old Testament and the God of the New Testament. The God of the Old Testament is very much the cosmic cop, while the God of the New Testament is loving and kind. This understanding can only come from a very shallow reading of the Bible. In reality, the writers of the Bible consistently portray God as both holy and loving, just and merciful. If there is a distinction between the Old Testament and the New Testament in relation to God's personality or nature, it has less to do with God than with the unfolding revelation of God's character that was only fully revealed in the person of Jesus.

3. C. S. Lewis, *The Lion, the Witch and the Wardrobe* (New York: Macmillan, 1950, 1981), 73–74.

Chapter 5

1. The life and teaching of Jesus is recorded in four independent biographical accounts, preserved in the Bible, which are named after their four authors: Matthew, Mark, Luke, and John. Extra-biblical sources supporting the historicity of Jesus include, but are not limited to, the writings of Thallus, a first-century Greek writer; Pliny the Younger (*Letters* 10.96); the Roman historians Tacitus (*Annals* 15.44) and Suetonius; and the Jewish historian Flavius Josephus (*Antiquities* 18.3.3). As Ian Wilson has noted, "Jesus is better documented than Shakespeare" (Ian Wilson, *Jesus: The Evidence* [New York: Harper and Row, 1996], 11). For an excellent introduction to the life and teaching of Jesus, beyond the four biographical accounts in the Bible, see Philip Yancey, *The Jesus I Never Knew* (Grand Rapids: Zondervan, 1995).

2. On the historical reliability of the Bible in regard to the sayings of Jesus, see chapter 8. The evidence supporting the accuracy of the Bible's record is staggering and has demonstrated that the life and teaching of Jesus as recorded in the Bible is based on firsthand, eyewitness accounts, some written as early as A.D. 50. On this, see Carsten Peter Thiede and Matthew D'Ancona, *Eyewitness to Jesus: Amazing New Manuscript Evidence about the Origin of the Gospels* (New York: Doubleday, 1996). For a full treatment of the reliability of the biblical text in relation to the teaching of Jesus, see C. Stephen Evans, *The Historical Christ and the Jesus of Faith: The Incarnational Narrative as History* (Oxford: Oxford University Press, 1996). This counters the work of the Jesus Seminar, a group of New Testament scholars who take a very skeptical view of the historical reliability of the Gospels in regard to the life and teaching of Jesus. For a specific critique of their work, see Ben Witherington III, *The Jesus Quest: The Third Search for the Jew of Nazareth* (Downers Grove, Ill.: InterVarsity Press, 1995); Michael J. Wilkins and J. P. Moreland, eds., *Jesus under Fire: Modern Scholarship Reinvents the Historical Jesus* (Grand Rapids: Zondervan, 1995); and Douglas Groothuis, *Searching for the Real Jesus in an Age of Controversy* (Eugene, Oreg.: Harvest House, 1996).

3. J. T. Fisher and L. S. Hawley, *A Few Buttons Missing* (Philadelphia: Lippincott, 1951), 273.

4. C. S. Lewis, *Mere Christianity* (New York: Macmillan, 1952), 40–41.

5. Many ask how Jesus could be God in human form but also the Son of God who prayed to his Father in heaven. To understand this is to understand the Trinity, an important Christian doctrine. In essence, the Trinity refers to the triune nature of God—he is three persons but one God. He is not three gods but three persons who are one God: God the Father, God the Son, and God the Holy Spirit. There are numerous references in the Bible that point to this aspect of God's nature (Matt. 3:16–17; Mark 1:10–11; John 14:16–17; 1 Cor. 12:4–6; 15:28; 2 Cor. 3:17; 4:4; 13:14; 1 Thess. 1:1; Heb. 1:2–3; and 1 Peter 1:2). Thus, Jesus was God the Son in human form. It should not be surprising that

the nature of God should extend beyond the limits of our faculties of understanding, for we are finite and God is infinite. But the ability to be three and one can still be found in our simplest elements, such as water. As water can be liquid, steam, and ice, yet remain the composite H_2O, so God can be three persons while remaining one God.

6. Yancey, *The Jesus I Never Knew,* 270.

Chapter 6

1. For a full treatment of this, see John R. W. Stott, *The Cross of Christ* (Downers Grove, Ill.: InterVarsity Press, 1986).

2. C. S. Lewis, *The Lion, the Witch and the Wardrobe* (New York: Macmillan, 1950, 1981), 156.

3. Adapted from Jack Canfield and Mark Victor Hansen, "On Courage," in *Chicken Soup for the Soul* (Deerfield Beach, Fla.: Health Communications, 1993), 27–28.

4. This illustration has been adapted from *The Bridge* (Colorado Springs: NavPress, 1981) by the Navigators, as well as Bill Hybels and Mark Mittelberg, *Becoming a Contagious Christian* (Grand Rapids: Zondervan/Willow Creek Resources, 1994), 156–59.

Chapter 7

1. In 1 Corinthians 15:6, the apostle Paul states that on one occasion Jesus appeared to over five hundred people. Paul boldly invites his readers to investigate the facts surrounding the resurrection for themselves, as most of the eyewitnesses were still alive to be queried.

2. Eusebius, for example, records the martyrdom of Peter; James, the brother of Jesus; and James, the brother of John.

3. Some attempt to explain this by claiming that the resurrection was really a symbolic event that the first Christians confused with a historical event. The difficulty with this perception is that the idea of the resurrection of Jesus in bodily form as an event in human history at a definite time and place was wildly

out of synch with established Jewish beliefs of the day. It would not have been a natural mistake for the disciples to have made in light of their background. Also, the idea that the resurrection was the result of some type of wish fulfillment is also problematic, as the history of Israel is littered with the corpses of pious Jewish martyrs, none of whom were ever thought of as having been raised from the dead. On this, see Alister McGrath, *Intellectuals Don't Need God and Other Modern Myths* (Grand Rapids: Zondervan, 1993), 120.

4. This idea was first suggested by Schleiermacher in 1799 but was not popularized until Hugh Schonfield's *The Passover Plot* (New York: Random House, 1965).

5. On the medical evidence that Jesus truly died as a result of his ordeal, see William D. Edwards, M.D., et al., "On the Physical Death of Jesus Christ," *Journal of the American Medical Association* 255, no. 11 (21 March 1986): 1463.

6. Pinchas Lapide, *The Resurrection of Jesus* (Minneapolis: Augsburg, 1983), 68.

7. For a helpful discussion on the plausibility of the miraculous, see C. S. Lewis, *Miracles* (New York: Collier Books, 1947, 1960).

8. The evidence surrounding the resurrection of Jesus is so overwhelming that a number of books have been devoted entirely to its reporting, such as the following: William Lane Craig, *Knowing the Truth about the Resurrection* (Ann Arbor: Servant, 1988); Stephen Davis, *Risen Indeed: Making Sense of the Resurrection* (Grand Rapids: Eerdmans, 1993); Michael Green, *The Day Death Died: Did Jesus Christ Really Rise from the Dead?* (Downers Grove, Ill.: InterVarsity Press, 1982); Gary Habermas and Anthony G. N. Flew, *Did Jesus Rise from the Dead?* ed. Terry L. Miethe (San Francisco: Harper and Row, 1987); and Frank Morison, *Who Moved the Stone?* (Grand Rapids: Zondervan, 1978). An excellent introduction to the vast material on the resurrection can be found in William Lane Craig's contribution to the aforementioned *Jesus under Fire*, "Did Jesus Rise from the Dead?" 141–76.

9. Adapted from Ida Mae Kempel, "What Was in Jeremy's Egg?" *Focus on the Family* (April 1988), 2–3.

Chapter 8

1. One of the best and most accessible overviews of Jesus' view of Scripture can be found in John R. W. Stott, *The Authority of the Bible* (Downers Grove, Ill.: InterVarsity Press, 1974).

2. See Luke 10:16; 1 Thess. 2:13.

3. The twenty-seven books of the New Testament were accepted as Scripture because they bore the mark of Jesus' authorization, which was apostolic origin. On the formation of the Bible, see F. F. Bruce, *The Canon of Scripture* (Downers Grove, Ill.: InterVarsity Press, 1988).

4. For further reading on the Bible's inspiration, see James Emery White, "Inspiration and Authority of Scripture," in *Foundations of Biblical Interpretation,* ed. David S. Dockery, Kenneth A. Matthews, and Robert B. Sloan (Nashville: Broadman and Holman, 1994), 19–35.

5. On the manuscript evidence surrounding these ancient documents, see F. F. Bruce, *The New Testament Documents: Are They Reliable?* 6th ed. (Grand Rapids: Eerdmans, 1984), 16–17.

6. Bruce M. Metzger, *Manuscripts of the Greek Bible* (New York: Oxford University Press, 1981), 54. Beyond these ancient Greek manuscripts, there are an additional eight thousand copies of the Latin Vulgate translation, along with other ancient manuscripts in Syriac and Coptic languages. See also Paul Barnett, *Is the New Testament Reliable?* (Downers Grove, Ill.: InterVarsity Press, 1986); F. F. Bruce, *The New Testament Documents*; and Josh McDowell, *Evidence That Demands a Verdict,* rev. ed. (San Bernardino, Calif.: Here's Life, 1979), 39–64.

7. For further study on this, see F. F. Bruce, *Second Thoughts on the Dead Sea Scrolls,* 2d ed. (Grand Rapids: Eerdmans, 1961); Millar Burrows, *Burrows on the Dead Sea Scrolls* (Grand Rapids: Baker, 1978); Philip R. Davies, *Qumran* (Grand Rapids: Eerdmans, 1982); William S. LaSor, *The Dead Sea Scrolls and the New Testament* (Grand Rapids: Eerdmans, 1972); Charles F. Pfeiffer, *The Dead Sea Scrolls and the Bible* (Grand Rapids: Baker, 1969); Hershel Shanks, ed., *Understanding the Dead Sea Scrolls* (New

York: Random House, 1992); R. de Vaux, *Archaeology and the Dead Sea Scrolls* (London: Oxford University Press, 1973); and Howard F. Vos, *Archaeology in Bible Lands* (New York: Simon and Schuster, 1957).

8. D. James Kennedy, *Why I Believe* (Dallas: Word, 1980), 33. On the historical reliability of the New Testament, see C. Stephen Evans, *The Historical Christ and the Jesus of Faith: The Incarnational Narrative as History* (Oxford: Oxford University Press, 1996), as well as Craig Blomberg's contribution to William Lane Craig, *Reasonable Faith* (Wheaton: Crossway, 1994), 193–231.

9. See Joseph P. Free, *Archaeology and Bible History,* revised and expanded by Howard F. Vos (Grand Rapids: Zondervan, 1992), 75, 114, 142.

10. Ibid., 16.

11. On this, see Howard F. Vos, *Archaeology in Bible Lands* (Chicago: Moody Press, 1977), 148. See also Free, *Archaeology and Bible History,* 57.

12. Free, *Archaeology and Bible History*, 108–9. For further study on the Hittites, see J. G. Macqueen, *The Hittites,* rev. ed. (London: Thames and Hudson, 1986).

13. Information gathered from John Noble Wilford, "Nonbiblical reference to King David Found," *The Charlotte Observer,* 6 August 1993, p. 17a. The integrity of this find was heightened by the fact that it was written by one of Israel's enemies who would have had every reason to want to ignore the reign of David.

14. Nelson Glueck, *Rivers in the Desert: History of Negev* (Philadelphia: Jewish Publications Society of America, 1969), 31. This assertion, despite countless archaeological discoveries related to the biblical record, continues to be true to date.

15. See Josh McDowell, "Why I Believe the Scripture," *Christian Herald* (March 1982), 45.

16. On this, see Carsten Peter Thiede and Matthew D'Ancona, *Eyewitness to Jesus: Amazing New Manuscript Evidence about the Origin of the Gospels* (New York: Doubleday, 1996). For a critique of the work of the Jesus Seminar, see Ben Witherington III, *The Jesus Quest: The Third Search for the Jew of Nazareth* (Downers

Grove, Ill.: InterVarsity Press, 1995); Michael J. Wilkins and J. P. Moreland, eds., *Jesus under Fire: Modern Scholarship Reinvents the Historical Jesus* (Grand Rapids: Zondervan, 1995); and Douglas Groothuis, *Searching for the Real Jesus in an Age of Controversy* (Eugene, Oreg.: Harvest House, 1996).

17. See F. F. Bruce, *The New Testament Documents: Are They Reliable?* See also C. Stephen Evans, *The Historical Christ and the Jesus of Faith.*

18. For example, in Isaiah 53, it was predicted that the Messiah would be rejected, would "carry our sorrows," and pay for our sins. In verse 5 of Isaiah 53, it even says that he would be "pierced" for our transgressions, which was hundreds of years before crucifixion had been developed as a method of execution. Isaiah 53 also predicts the Messiah coming back to life after his death (v. 11). Other prophetic passages include, but are not limited to, Psalm 22 and Micah 5:2.

19. Peter W. Stoner, *Science Speaks* (Chicago: Moody Press, 1969), 107–9.

20. It is my understanding that this number was first established by F. E. Hamilton, *The Basis of Christian Faith*, 3d ed. (New York: Harper and Row, 1946), 156.

21. As calculated by Lee Strobel, *Inside the Mind of Unchurched Harry and Mary* (Grand Rapids: Zondervan, 1995), 37.

22. There is little doubt, however, that there are certain passages that need additional study and reflection. For helpful discussion of such passages, see Gleason L. Archer, *Encyclopedia of Bible Difficulties* (Grand Rapids: Zondervan, 1982); W. Arndt, *Does the Bible Contradict Itself?* 5th ed. (St. Louis: Concordia Publishing House, 1955); and Walter C. Kaiser Jr., Peter H. Davids, F. F. Bruce, and Manfred T. Brauch, *Hard Sayings of the Bible* (Downers Grove, Ill.: InterVarsity Press, 1996). Also helpful would be one of the many good one-volume Bible handbooks, such as the *Holman Bible Handbook* (Nashville: Broadman and Holman, 1992), of which the author served as consulting editor and contributing author.

23. According to David S. Dockery, what Christians mean by the truth of the Bible is "the idea that when all the facts are known,

the Bible (in its autographs, that is, the original documents), properly interpreted in light of the culture and the means of communication that had developed by the time of its composition, is completely true in all that it affirms, to the degree of precision intended by the authors' purpose, in all matters relating to God and His creation." On this, see David S. Dockery, *Christian Scripture* (Nashville: Broadman and Holman, 1995), 64. A similar definition can be found in Millard Erickson, *Christian Theology,* 1-vol. ed. (Grand Rapids: Baker, 1983, 1984, 1985), 233–34.

24. This analogy has been adapted from Lee Strobel, *Inside the Mind of Unchurched Harry and Mary*, 115–16.

Chapter 9

1. Adapted from Ricki Morell, "An Evening's Flight—to Tragedy," *The Charlotte Observer,* 10 July 1994, pp. 1A, 11A.

2. Adapted from Kevin Johnson, "Family's Painful Question: 'Why?'" *USA Today,* 21 April 1997, p. 4A.

3. As cited by Philip Yancey, *Disappointment with God* (Grand Rapids: Zondervan, 1988), 179.

4. C. S. Lewis, *A Grief Observed* (San Francisco: Harper and Row, 1961), 10–11.

5. For further reading on this issue, see Peter Kreeft, *Making Sense Out of Suffering* (Ann Arbor: Servant, 1986); C. S. Lewis, *The Problem of Pain* (London: Geoffrey Bless, 1940); and Philip Yancey, *Where Is God When It Hurts?* (Grand Rapids: Zondervan, 1978).

6. Yancey, *Where Is God When It Hurts?,* 51.

7. Ibid., 56.

8. James Dobson, *When God Doesn't Make Sense* (Wheaton: Tyndale, 1993), 193.

9. Lewis, *Problem of Pain,* 22. Not only is there the "good" of free will, but there can be a positive element to pain. C. S. Lewis called it the "megaphone" of God, which arrests our attention; Dr. Paul Brand applauds its benefits for physical defense and early warning system to our bodies; James Dobson and Philip Yancey note its use for faith development. But it must never be seen, in

and of itself, as good, only able to be used by God for good in spite of its tragic nature.

10. C. S. Lewis, *The Four Loves* (New York: Harcourt, Brace and World, 1960), 169.

11. As cited by Billy Graham, *Hope for the Troubled Heart* (Dallas: Word, 1991), 44–45.

12. Joni has written a biography of her life, simply titled *Joni* (New York: Bantam, 1976).

13. On this, see Os Guinness, *God in the Dark: The Assurance of Faith beyond a Shadow of Doubt* (Wheaton: Crossway, 1996), 178ff.

14. Adapted from Dobson, *When God Doesn't Make Sense*, 222–23.

Chapter 10

1. Malise Ruthven, *The Divine Supermarket: Shopping for God in America* (New York: William Morrow, 1989).

2. For this idea, see Rabbi Marc Gellman and Monsignor Thomas Hartman, *How Do You Spell God?* (New York: Morrow Junior Books, 1995), 19–24.

3. America's pluralism has been fueled largely through the twin dynamics of religious freedom and complete equality of all religious groups before the civil law. On this, see Sydney E. Mead, *The Lively Experiment: The Shaping of Christianity in America* (New York: Harper and Row, 1963). See also Nathan O. Hatch, *The Democratization of American Christianity* (New Haven: Yale University Press, 1989).

4. For an excellent overview of world religions, see Mircea Eliade and Ioan P. Couliano, with Hillary S. Wiesner, *The Eliade Guide to World Religions* (New York: HarperSanFrancisco, 1991); and R. C. Zaehner, ed., *The Concise Encyclopedia of Living Faiths* (Boston: Beacon Press, 1959).

5. Adapted from Michael Green and Gordon Carkner, *Ten Myths about Christianity* (Batavia, Ill.: Lion Publishing, 1988), 71.

6. On this, see Alister McGrath, *Explaining Your Faith* (Grand Rapids: Baker, 1995), 132.

7. On this, see Paul Little, *Know Why You Believe* (Downers Grove, Ill.: InterVarsity Press, 1988), 152.

8. Adapted from Cliff Knechtle, *Give Me an Answer* (Downers Grove, Ill.: InterVarsity Press, 1986), 28–29.

9. C. S. Lewis, *Mere Christianity* (New York: Macmillan, 1952), 29.

10. George Barna, *What Americans Believe* (Ventura, Calif.: Regal, 1991), 83.

11. Allan Bloom, *The Closing of the American Mind* (New York: Simon and Schuster, 1987), 25.

12. Robert N. Bellah, Richard Madsen, William M. Sullivan, Ann Swidler, and Steven M. Tipton, *Habits of the Heart: Individualism and Commitment in American Life* (New York: Harper and Row, 1985), 220–21.

13. For an overview of the correspondence theory of truth, see A. N. Prior, "Correspondence Theory of Truth," *The Encyclopedia of Philosophy,* vol. 2, ed. Paul Edwards (New York: Macmillan and The Free Press, 1967), 223–32. On the concept of truth in the Bible, see Anthony C. Thiselton, "Truth," *The New International Dictionary of New Testament Theology,* vol. 3, ed. Colin Brown (Grand Rapids: Regency/Zondervan, 1986), 874–902. The classical understanding of the correspondence theory of truth can be found in the writings of Aristotle, such as "Metaphysica," trans. W. D. Ross, *The Great Books of the Western World,* vol. 8, ed. Robert Maynard Hutchins (Chicago: Encyclopaedia Britannica, Inc., 1952), 1011.b.26ff.; "Categoriae," trans. E. M. Edghill, *The Great Books of the Western World,* vol. 8, ed. Robert Maynard Hutchins (Chicago: Encyclopaedia Britannica, Inc., 1952), 4.a.10–4.b.19; and "De interpretatione," trans. E. M. Edghill, *The Great Books of the Western World,* vol. 8, ed. Robert Maynard Hutchins (Chicago: Encyclopaedia Britannica, Inc., 1952), 16.a.10–19.

14. Unless, of course, you want to deny the reliability of our senses and posit that we are removed from any understanding of true reality. This, however, leads to nothing but intellectual nihilism.

For a full treatment of the concept of truth in Christian thought, see the author's *What Is Truth?* (Nashville: Broadman and Holman, 1994).

15. As quoted in *Great Books of the Western World,* vol. 3, ed. Robert Maynard Hutchins, 915. On the idea of truth in Christian thought, see the author's *What Is Truth?* (Nashville: Broadman and Holman, 1994).

16. For further study, see Harold A. Netland, *Dissonant Voices: Religious Pluralism and the Question of Truth* (Grand Rapids: Eerdmans, 1991).

17. On this, see David Yount, *Growing in Faith: A Guide for the Reluctant Christian* (Washington: Regnery, 1994), 302.

18. As quoted by Will and Ariel Durant, *The Lessons of History* (New York: Simon and Schuster, 1968), 51.

19. On this, see the Book of Romans, specifically chapters 1 and 2.

20. Lewis, *Mere Christianity,* 50.

Chapter 11

1. Adapted from Robert Fulghum, *It Was on Fire When I Lay Down on It* (New York: Villard Books, 1989), 9–15.

2. On this, see Elton Trueblood, *The Humor of Christ* (New York: Harper and Row, 1964).

3. Adapted from Ken Blanchard, *We Are the Beloved: A Spiritual Journey* (Grand Rapids: Zondervan, 1994), 19–20.

4. Bill Wolfe, "Church Meeting Ends in Fray, Beleaguered Pastor Resigns Amid Turmoil," *The Courier-Journal,* 10 December 1990, p. 1A.

5. Adapted from Gordon Aeschliman, *Cages of Pain: Healing for Disillusioned Christians* (Dallas: Word, 1991), 24–26.

6. Adapted from Gordon MacDonald, *The Life God Blesses* (Nashville: Thomas Nelson, 1994), 59.

7. Adapted from C. S. Lewis, *Mere Christianity* (New York: Macmillan, 1952), 163.

8. This analogy has been borrowed and adapted from C. S. Lewis.

9. For a full description of the church as the new community and how church might be "rethought" in light of some of the concerns mentioned, see the author's *Rethinking the Church* (Grand Rapids: Baker, 1997).

10. I do not know where I first heard this analogy, but it is far from original with me and has appeared in a number of forms in numerous messages and books.

11. As cited by A. N. Wilson, *The Lion and the Honeycomb: The Religious Writings of Leo Tolstoy* (San Francisco: Harper and Row, 1987), 148.

Chapter 12

1. Adapted from John Ortberg, *The Life You've Always Wanted* (Grand Rapids: Zondervan, 1997), 24–28.

Chapter 13

1. See Paul Brand and Philip Yancey, *In His Image* (Grand Rapids: Zondervan, 1984), 227–29.

2. Adapted from Charles R. Swindoll, *Growing Strong in the Seasons of Life* (Portland, Oreg.: Multnomah, 1983), 48–49.

3. Source unknown.

Chapter 14

1. This summary was adapted from Henrietta C. Mears, *What the Bible Is All About,* rev. ed. (Ventura, Calif.: Regal, 1983), 23. For more on the message of the Bible and the significance of Jesus' life, death, and resurrection, see chapters 5, 6, and 7 of this book.

James Emery White is the founding and senior pastor of Mecklenburg Community Church in Charlotte, North Carolina. Started in a Hilton hotel in October of 1992, Mecklenburg is often cited as one of the fastest growing church starts in the United States, experiencing over 80 percent of its growth from the unchurched. This has generated widespread media attention, including reports by the *CBS Evening News* and *USA Today*. Jim previously served as the leadership consultant for preaching and worship for the Southern Baptist Convention.

Mecklenburg adheres to a unique philosophy of ministry. On weekends, drama, multimedia, contemporary music, and practical messages are used to present the timeless truths of Scripture at an introductory level easily understood by nonchurched people.

Dr. White holds the B.S. degree in public relations and business from Appalachian State University, and the M.Div. and Ph.D. degrees from the Southern Baptist Theological Seminary, where he was awarded a Garrett Teaching Fellowship in both New Testament and theology. He has also done advanced graduate study in American religious history at Vanderbilt University. He has served as a visiting professor at such institutions as the Southern Baptist Theological Seminary, the Southeastern Baptist Theological Seminary, and the Moscow Theological Institute. He is currently adjunctive professor of Christian theology at Gordon-Conwell Theological Seminary and serves on the president's advisory council of Union University.

Jim and his wife, Susan, live in Charlotte, where they homeschool their four children, Rebecca, Rachel, Jonathan, and Zachary.

Steps to Peace with God

Step 1 God's Purpose:
Peace and Life

God loves you and wants you to experience peace and
life—abundant and eternal.

The Bible Says . . .

"... we have peace with God through our Lord
Jesus Christ." Romans 5:1

"For God so loved the world that He gave His
only begotten Son, that whoever believes in Him
should not perish but have everlasting life."
John 3:16

"... I have come that they may have life,
and that they may have it more abundantly."
John 10:10b

Since God planned
for us to have peace
and the abundant life
right now, why are
most people not hav-
ing this experience?

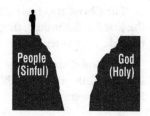

Step 2 Our Problem:
Separation

God created us in His own image to have an abundant
life. He did not make us as robots to automatically love
and obey Him, but gave us a will and a freedom of
choice.

We chose to disobey God and go our own willful way.
We still make this choice today. This results in separation from God.

The Bible Says . . .

"For all have sinned and fall short of the glory
of God." Romans 3:23

"For the wages of sin is death, but the gift of
God is eternal life in Christ Jesus our Lord."
Romans 6:23

Our choice results
in separation from
God.

Our Attempts

There is only on remedy for this prob lem of separation.

Through the ages, individuals have tried in many ways to bridge this gap . . . without success . . .

The Bible Says . . .

"There is a way that seems right to man, but in the end it leads to death." Proverbs 14:12

"But your iniquities have separated you from God; and your sins have hidden His face from you, so that He will not hear." Isaiah 59:2

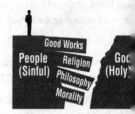

Step 3 God's Remedy: The Cross

Jesus Christ is the only answer to this problem. He died on the Cross and rose from the grave, paying the penalty for our sin and bridging the gap between God and people.

The Bible Says . . .

". . . God is on one side and all the people on the other side, and Christ Jesus, Himself man, is between them to bring them together . . ." 1 Timothy 2:5

"For Christ also has suffered once for sins, the just for the unjust, that He might bring us to God . . ." 1 Peter 3:18a

"But God demonstrates His own love for us in this: While we were still sinners, Christ died for us." Romans 5:8

God has provided the only way . . . we must make the choice . . .

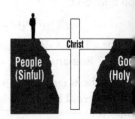

Step 4 | Our Response:
Receive Christ

...e must trust Jesus Christ and receive Him by personal ...itation.

The Bible Says . . .

"Behold, I stand at the door and knock. If ...yone hears My voice and opens the door, I ...ll come in to him and dine with him, and he ...th Me." Revelation 3:20

"But as many as received Him, to them He ...ve the right to become children of God, even ... those who believe in His name." John 1:12

". . . if you confess with your mouth the ...rd Jesus and believe in your heart that God ...s raised Him from the dead, you will be saved." ...mans 10:9

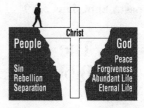

Are you here . . . or here?

...there any good reason why you cannot receive Jesus Christ right now?

How to receive Christ:

Admit your need (I am a sinner).

Be willing to turn from your sins (repent).

Believe that Jesus Christ died for you on the Cross and rose from the grave.

Through prayer, invite Jesus Christ to come in and control your life through the Holy Spirit. (Receive Him as Lord and Savior.)

What to Pray:

...ear Lord Jesus,

I know that I am a sinner and need Your forgiveness. I believe that You ...ed for my sins. I want to turn from my sins. I now invite You to come into ...y heart and life. I want to trust and follow You as Lord and Savior.

In Jesus' name. Amen.

_____   _____
Date   Signature

God's Assurance: His Word

If you prayed this prayer,

The Bible Says...

"For 'whoever calls upon the name of the Lord will be saved.'"
Romans 10:13

Did you sincerely ask Jesus Christ to come into your life? Where is He right now? What has He given you?

"For it is by grace you have been saved, through faith—and this is not from yourselves, it is the gift of God—not by works, so that no one can boast." **Ephesians 2:8,9**

The Bible Says...

"He who has the Son has life; he who does not have the Son of God does not have life. These things I have written to you who believe in the name of the Son of God, that you may know that you have eternal life, and that you may continue to believe in the name of the Son of God." **1 John 5:12–13, NKJV**

Receiving Christ, we are born into God's family through the supernatural work of the Holy Spirit who indwells every believer...this is called regeneration or the "new birth."

This is just the beginning of a wonderful new life in Christ. To deepen this relationship you should:

1. Read your Bible every day to know Christ better.
2. Talk to God in prayer every day.
3. Tell others about Christ.
4. Worship, fellowship, and serve with other Christians in a church where Christ is preached.
5. As Christ's representative in a needy world, demonstrate your new life by your love and concern for others.

God bless you as you do.

Billy Graham

If you want further help in the decision you have made, write to:
Billy Graham Evangelistic Association P.O. Box 779, Minneapolis, Minnesota 55440-0779